KU-335-736

The **AA POCKET**Guide

ANDALUCÍA

Andalucía: Regions and Best places to see

 Best places to see 20–41

 Featured sight

 Córdoba and Jaén Provinces 45–59

 Málaga and Cádiz Provinces 80–99

 Granada and Almería Provinces 60–79

 Seville and Huelva Provinces 100–113

Original text by Des Hannigan
Updated by Robin Barton

© AA Media Limited 2008.
First published 2008. Reprinted April 2011.

ISBN: 978-0-7495-5745-4

Published by AA Publishing, a trading name of AA Media Limited, whose registered office is Fanum House, Basing View, Basingstoke, Hampshire RG21 4EA. Registered number 06112600.

AA Media Limited retains the copyright in the original edition © 2000 and in all subsequent editions, reprints and amendments.

A CIP catalogue record for this book is available from the British Library.

We have tried to ensure accuracy in this guide, but things do change, so please let us know if you have any comments at travelguides@theAA.com.

Colour separation: Keenes, Andover
Printed and bound in Italy by Printer Trento S.r.l.
Front cover images: (t) AA/M Chaplow; (b) AA/J Edmanson
Back cover image: AA/M Chaplow

A04690
Maps in this title produced from mapping © ISTITUTO GEOGRAFICO DE AGOSTINI S.p.A., NOVARA 2007

About this book

This book is divided into four sections.

Planning pages 6–19
Before you go; Getting there; Getting
around; Being there

Best places to see pages 20–41
The unmissable highlights of any visit
to Andalucía

Exploring pages 42–113
The best places to visit in Andalucía,
organized by area

Maps pages 117–127
All map references are to the atlas
section. For example, Granada has the
reference ✚ 124 D4 – indicating the
page number and the grid square in
which it can be found

Addresses c/ = Calle (Street)
s/n = sin numero (no number)

Contents

Planning

Before you go

WHEN TO GO

JAN	FEB	MAR	APR	MAY	JUN	JUL	AUG	SEP	OCT	NOV	DEC
16°C	17°C	18°C	21°C	23°C	27°C	29°C	29°C	27°C	23°C	19°C	17°C
61°F	63°F	64°F	70°F	73°F	81°F	84°F	84°F	81°F	73°F	66°F	63°F

High season   Low season

Andalucía has a Mediterranean climate: hot, dry summers and mild, wet winters. However, the climate varies by geography as well as the season. Generally, the coast to the west is windier and wetter, with weather fronts sweeping in off the Atlantic, while the east of Andalucía is dry to the extent of desertification around Almería. Low-lying inland areas, such as Seville and Córdoba, get extremely hot in July and August but mountain regions can remain cool until well into the summer; in the winter the mountains are usually cold and wet and often snowbound.

Consider when local festivals are taking place – it is very hard to find accommodation during festivals such as *Semana Santa* (Holy Week) in Seville. In the winter many coastal resorts close down for a month or two.

WHAT YOU NEED

● Required
○ Suggested
▲ Not required

Some countries require a passport to remain valid for a minimum period (usually at least six months) beyond the date of entry – contact their consulate or embassy or your travel agency for details.

	UK	Germany	USA	Netherlands
Passport (or National Identity Card where applicable)	●	●	●	●
Visa (regulations can change – check before your journey)	▲	▲	▲	▲
Onward or Return Ticket	▲	▲	▲	▲
Health Inoculations	▲	▲	▲	▲
Health Documentation (► 9, Health Insurance)	●	●	●	●
Travel Insurance	○	○	○	○
Driving Licence (national – EU format/Spanish translation/international)	●	●	●	●
Car Insurance Certificate (if own car)	●	●	●	●
Car Registration Document (if own car)	●	●	●	●

WEBSITES

www.spain.info
Spain's national tourist office

www.andalucia.org
Regional tourism website

TOURIST OFFICES AT HOME

In the UK

Spanish Tourist Office,
22/23 Manchester Square,
London W1M 5AP
☎ 020 7486 8077

In the USA

Tourist Office of Spain,

35th Floor, 666 Fifth Avenue,
New York, NY 10103
☎ 212 265 8822
and
Tourist Office of Spain,
8383 Wilshire Boulevard,
Suite 960, Beverley Hills, CA 90211
☎ 323 658 7188

HEALTH INSURANCE

EU nationals can get reduced-cost emergency medical treatment with the
European Health Insurance Card (EHIC), although medical insurance is still
advised and is essential for all other visitors. Visitors from the US should
check their insurance coverage.

ADVANCE PASSENGER INFORMATION

Security rules introduced in June 2007 mean that all passengers on all
flights to and from Spain must now supply Advance Passenger
Information (API) to the Spanish authorities: full given names, surname,
nationality, date of birth and travel document details (passport number).
Airlines will be responsible for collecting the compulsory information
either through their websites, travel agents, or airport check-in desks.

TIME DIFFERENCES

GMT	Spain	Germany	USA (NY)	Netherlands	Italy
12 noon	1PM	1PM	7AM	1PM	1PM

Spain is one hour ahead of Greenwich Mean Time (GMT+1) in winter,
but summer time (GMT+2) operates from late March until late October.

PLANNING

NATIONAL HOLIDAYS

1 Jan *New Year's Day*

6 Jan *Epiphany*

28 Feb *Andalucían Day (regional)*

Mar/Apr *Maundy Thursday, Good Friday, Easter Monday*

1 May *Labour Day*

24 Jun *San Juan (regional)*

25 Jul *Santiago (regional)*

15 Aug *Assumption of the Virgin*

12 Oct *National Day*

1 Nov *All Saints' Day*

6 Dec *Constitution Day*

8 Dec *Feast of the Immaculate Conception*

25 Dec *Christmas Day*

WHAT'S ON WHEN

January 6 Jan: *Cabalgata de los Reyes Magos*, Málaga. An Epiphany parade.

February Pre-Lenten, week-long *Carnaval* in many Andalucían towns and cities, including Antequera, Cádiz, Carmona, Córdoba, Málaga.

March/April *Semana Santa* (Holy Week). Follows Palm Sunday and is one of the most powerful and passionate celebrations in the world. It is most colourful and dramatic in Seville.

April This is the month of the most exuberant *ferias* – Seville's is among the best and biggest in Spain. It is held one or two weeks after Easter, but always in April. Vejer de la Frontera holds an Easter Sunday *feria*, with bull-running through the streets.

May First week: Horse Fair, Jerez de la Frontera.

Fiesta de los Patios. Córdoba's fabulous private patios are open to the public in early May.

First weekend of May: *Las Cruces de Mayo*. Córdoba's most popular festival, with street dancing and fully booked hotels.

Romería del Rocío (Whitsun). Vast numbers congregate at the village of El Rocío, Huelva, to celebrate the *La Blanca Paloma*, the 'White Dove', the Virgen del Rocío.

Thursday after Trinity Sunday: *Corpus Christi*. Festivals and bullfights in Seville, Granada, Ronda, Zahara de la Sierra, and at smaller towns.

June Second week: *Feria de San Barnabé*, Marbella.

13–14 Jun: *Fiesta de San Antonio*, Trevélez, Las Alpujarras. Mock battles between Moors and Christians.

July *La Virgen del Carmen*, Fuengirola, Estepona, Marbella, Nerja and Torremolinos. Celebrates the patron saint of fishermen.

August 5 Aug: *Mulhacén Romería*, Trevélez. Midnight procession to Sierra Nevada's highest peak.

13–21 Aug: *Feria de Málaga*. Very lively fiesta.

Mid-Aug: Horse races along the sandy beaches at Sanlúcar de Barrameda.

Third weekend: *Fiesta de San Mames*, Aroche. Friendly village fiesta.

September 7 Sep: *Romería del Cristo de la Yedra*, Baeza. Street processions and entertainment.

6–13 Sep: *Festival Vírgen de la Luz*, Tarifa.

First two weeks: *Feria de Pedro Romero*, Ronda. Celebration of the famous bullfighter.

October 15–23 Oct: *Feria de San Lucas*, Jaén. The city's main festival.

6–12 Oct: *Feria del Rosario*, Fuengirola. Horse riding and flamenco.

December 28 Dec: *Fiesta de los Verdiales*, Málaga province. Lively, theatrical and musical event in villages to the north of Málaga.

Pride and Passion

The *festival* (festival), the *feria* (fair) and the *fiesta* (holiday) are at the heart of Andalucían culture. The *festival* is often religious in its elements. The *feria* originates from livestock fairs and today is significant for much flamboyant horsemanship. *Romerías* are religious processions culminating in a picnic. The line between the religious and the secular is blurred in Andalucía, and the same earthy passion is expressed during the most intense religious periods, such as Holy Week, as at the life-affirming spring celebrations. Celebration is so inherent to life in Andalucía that visitors are likely to find themselves with some form of local *feria* or *festival* due in their locality. Do not miss out on them if you want to get near to the absolute, exuberant, passionate essence of Andalucía.

Getting there

BY AIR

Almería Airport

10km (6 miles) to city centre

- 25 minutes
- 20 minutes
- 20 minutes

Málaga Airport

10km (6 miles) to city centre

- 12 minutes
- 20 minutes
- 20 minutes

Seville Airport

8km (5 miles) to city centre

- N/A
- 20 minutes
- 20 minutes

Andalucía's principal airports are Málaga and Seville, with low-cost airlines also flying to Almería and Granada. Málaga's airport is the region's largest and will double in size by 2010, with the addition of new terminal buildings and a new runway. The work taking place at Málaga will cause delays to those driving to the airport, so factor in extra time to negotiate the traffic. New security measures introduced to Spanish airports in 2006 and 2007 may slow down check-in times; confirm the current regulations with your airline before setting off for the airport.

Most of Spain's airports are managed by Aena (☎ 902 404 704; www.aena.es); in Andalucía these airports are Almería, Córdoba, Granada, Jerez, Málaga and Seville. Updates, flight information and airport maps can be downloaded from the organization's website.

Flights to Andalucía from various British airports, including London's Heathrow, Gatwick, Luton and Stansted airports, and Bristol, Bournemouth, Southampton, Manchester, Glasgow and Birmingham take less than three hours. Many other European countries have direct flights to Andalucían airports, but flights from North America will be routed via

Madrid. Fares for budget airline flights from Europe will typically be less expensive than the corresponding rail fare or the cost of driving; there may also be favourable car rental rates from the airline. Package holidays booked through an agent are another option, although these are diminishing in popularity due to number of self-booked holidays that can be found on the internet.

BY CAR

Outside of the cities and the fast, narrow A7 coast road, driving in Andalucía can be enjoyable. Fast, well-maintained motorways (A-roads) connect Andalucía with Madrid, Valencia and other major cities.

BY TRAIN

Reaching Andalucía by train typically involves taking a train from Madrid to Seville or Córdoba. Spain's extensive train network, operated by RENFE (www.renfe.es), is one of the least expensive in Europe. Tickets can be purchased in advance from travel agents, from RENFE's website or at rail stations. A train journey from the UK to Andalucía will take more than 24 hours and will involve several changes – at least at Paris and Madrid.

BY FERRY

There are ferry services to Bilbao and Santander, on Spain's northwest coast, from the British ports of Plymouth and Portsmouth. A crossing typically takes between 24 and 34 hours in a car ferry operated by P&O Ferries (www.poferries.com) or Brittany Ferries (www.brittany-ferries.co.uk). You then need to drive through western and central Spain to reach Andalucía. There are also ferry services from Tangier, Ceuta and Melilla in Morocco to Tarifa, Algeciras, Málaga, Motril, Almería and Gibraltar.

Getting around

PUBLIC TRANSPORT

Internal Flights The national airline, Iberia (www.iberia.com), plus the smaller Aviaco, operate an extensive network of internal flights. For reservations on domestic flights ☎ 902 40 05 00.

Trains Services are provided by the state-run company – RENFE (www.renfe.es). Fares are usually relatively inexpensive. For rail inquiries for Almería ☎ 950 23 18 22; for Cádiz, Córdoba, Granada, Seville and Málaga ☎ 902 24 02 02 (this line has an English-language option).

Buses Andalucía has a comprehensive and reliable bus network operated by different companies along the coast and to inland towns and villages. Fares are very reasonable. Go to the local bus station for details of routes: Almería ☎ 950 26 20 98; Cádiz ☎ 950 21 00 29; Córdoba ☎ 957 40 40 40; Granada ☎ 958 18 54 80; Seville ☎ 954 41 71 11; Málaga ☎ 952 35 00 61.

Urban Transport Traffic in the cities of Andalucía generally, and in the main towns and resorts of the Costa del Sol in particular, is normally heavy, especially in summer, but public transport in the form of buses is generally good.

TAXIS

Only use taxis that display a licence issued by the local authority. Taxis show a green light when available for hire. They can be flagged down in the street. In cities and large towns taxis are metered; where they are not, agree the price of the journey in advance.

FARES AND TICKETS

Train services are categorized according to the speed of the service: the high-speed AVE trains serve just Córdoba and Seville in Andalucía while slower, regional services connect smaller towns and cities. Train tickets can be purchased in advance online at www.renfe.es, or from travel agents. Collect your pre-purchased ticket from a station; bring ID and the credit card you used to make the booking. It is worth booking in advance for long-distance trips at peak times on popular tourist routes. Tickets can also be purchased from counters and machines in stations.

Bus services are managed by numerous local companies; timetables are available from local tourist offices and tickets can be purchased at the point of travel. Buses are a good way of travelling from village to village but trains are preferable for journeys of an hour or longer.

DRIVING

- Speed limits on *autopistas* (toll motorways) and *autovías* (free motorways): 120kph (74mph); dual carriageways and roads with overtaking lanes: 100kph (62mph).
- Speed limits on country roads: 90kph (56mph).
- Speed limits on urban roads: 50kph (31mph); in residential areas: 20kph (12mph).
- Take care on the N340 coastal highway – a particularly dangerous road.
- Seatbelts must be worn in front seats at all times and in rear seats where fitted.
- Random breath-testing. Never drive under the influence of alcohol.
- Fuel (*gasolina*) is available as either *sin plomo* (unleaded, 95 and 98 octane) or *gasoleo/gasoil* (diesel). Petrol prices are fixed by the government and are lower than those in the UK. Most garages take credit cards.
- If you break down in your own car and are a member of an AIT-affiliated motoring club, call the Real Automóvil Club de España, or RACE (☎ 915 94 74 00; www.race.es) for assistance. If the car is hired you should follow the instructions in the documentation; most international rental firms provide a rescue service.

CAR RENTAL

The leading international car rental companies operate in the main cities and on the Costa del Sol. You can hire a car in advance (essential at peak periods) either direct or through a travel agent.

Being there

TOURIST OFFICES

Almería
Parque Nicolás Salmerón s/n
☎ 950 27 43 55

Baeza
Plaza del Pópulo s/n
☎ 953 74 04 44

Cádiz
Avenida Ramón de Carranza s/n
☎ 956 25 86 46

Córdoba
c/ Torrijos 10 ☎ 957 47 12 35

Granada
Corral del Carbón,
c/ Libreras 2 ☎ 958 22 59 90
Municipal Tourist Office:
Plaza Mariana Pineda 10
☎ 958 24 71 28

Huelva
Avenida de Alemania 12
☎ 959 25 74 03

Jaén
Maestra 13 ☎ 953 24 26 24

Málaga
Pasaje de Chinitas 4
☎ 952 21 34 45

Ronda
Plaza de España 1 ☎ 952 87 12 72

Seville
Avda de Kansas City s/n, Estación
de Santa Justa ☎ 954 53 76 26

Úbeda
Bajo de Marqués 4 ☎ 954 75 08 97

MONEY

Spain's currency is the euro, which is divided into 100 cents. Coins come in denominations of 1, 2, 5, 10, 20 and 50 cents, 1 and 2 euros, and notes come in 5, 10, 20, 50, 100, 200 and 500 euro denominations.

TIPS/GRATUITIES

Yes ✓ No ✗		
Restaurants (if service not included)	✓	5–10%
Cafés/Bars (if service not included)	✓	change
Taxis	✓	2–3%
Chambermaids/Porters	✓	change
Toilets	✓	change

POSTAL SERVICES

Post offices (*correos*) are generally open Mon–Fri
9–2, Sat 9–1; in main centres they may open for
longer. Málaga's main post office is at Avenida de
Andalucía 1 (☎ 902 197 197; www.correos.es).
Stamps (*sellos*) can also be bought at tobacconists
(*estancos*).

TELEPHONES

All telephone numbers throughout Spain now consist of
nine digits and you must always dial all nine digits. Local
calls are inexpensive. Although you can pay with coins,
it is quicker and easier to buy a phonecard from any
estanco (tobacconist). Many phones also take credit
cards. Long-distance calls are cheaper from a booth than
from your hotel. Directory information is 003.

International Dialling Codes

From Spain to:	
UK: 00 44	USA: 00 1
Germany: 00 49	Netherlands: 00 31
	Ireland: 00 353

INTERNET SERVICES

Many mid- and high-priced hotels offer some sort of internet access.
Most towns and cities have at least one internet café, but wireless
broadband (wi-fi) is less common than in some countries. Expect to pay
for internet access in hotels and cafés, but rates should be reasonable.

EMBASSIES AND CONSULATES

UK ☎ 952 352 300 (Málaga)   Netherlands ☎ 952 27 99 54
Germany ☎ 952 21 24 42 (Málaga)   (Málaga)
Ireland ☎ 954 21 63 61 (Seville)   USA ☎ 952 47 48 91 (Fuengirola)

HEALTH ADVICE

Sun Advice Try to avoid the midday sun and always use a high-factor sun
cream. The sunniest months are July and August, when daytime
temperatures often reach more than 30°C (86°F).

Medicines Prescriptions, non-prescription drugs and medicines are available from pharmacies (*farmácias*), distinguished by a large green cross. They are able to dispense many drugs that would be available only on prescription in other countries.

Safe Water Tap water is chlorinated and generally safe to drink; however, unfamiliar water may cause mild abdominal upsets. Mineral water (*agua mineral*) is inexpensive and widely available. It is sold *sin gas* (still) and *con gas* (carbonated).

PERSONAL SAFETY

Snatching of handbags and cameras, pick-pocketing, theft of unattended baggage and car break-ins are the principal crimes against visitors. Any crime or loss should be reported to the national police force (Policía Nacional), who wear blue uniforms.

Some precautions:

● Do not leave valuables on the beach or poolside.
● Place valuables in a hotel safety-deposit box.
● Wear handbags and cameras across your chest.
● Avoid lonely, seedy and dark areas at night.

ELECTRICITY

The power supply is 220/230 volts (in some bathrooms and older buildings it is 110/120 volts). Buildings have round two-hole sockets taking round plugs of two round pins. British visitors will need an adaptor and US visitors a voltage transformer.

OPENING HOURS

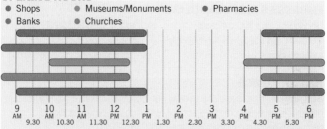

● Shops   ● Museums/Monuments   ● Pharmacies
● Banks   ● Churches

LANGUAGE

Spanish is one of the easiest languages. All vowels are pure and short. Some useful tips on speaking: 'c' is lisped before 'e' and 'i', otherwise hard; 'h' is silent; 'j' is pronounced like a gutteral 'j'; 'r' is rolled; 'v' sounds more like 'b'; and 'z' is the same as a soft 'c'. English is widely spoken in the principal resorts but you will get a better reception if you at least try communicating with Spaniards in their own tongue.

hotel	*hotel*	reservation	*reserva*
room	*habitación*	rate	*precio*
single/double	*individual/doble*	breakfast	*desayuno*
one/two nights	*una/dos noche(s)*	toilet	*lavabo*
per person	*por persona*	bath	*baño*
per room	*por habitación*	shower	*ducha*
bank	*banco*	coin	*moneda*
exchange office	*oficina de cambio*	foreign currency	*moneda extranjera*
post office	*correos*	change money	*cambiar dinero*
cashier	*cajero*	pound sterling	*libra esterlina*
money	*dinero*	American dollar	*dólar americano*
restaurant	*restaurante*	tourist menu	*menú turístico*
bar	*bar*	wine list	*carta de vinos*
table	*mesa*	lunch	*almuerzo*
menu	*carta*	dinner	*cena*
aeroplane	*avión*	bus stop	*parada de autobús*
airport	*aeropuerto*	ticket	*billete*
flight	*vuelo*	single/return	*ida/ida y vuelta*
train	*tren*	timetable	*horario*
train station	*estación ferrocarril*	non-smoking	*no fumadores*
yes	*sí*	goodbye	*adiós*
no	*no*	good night	*buenas noches*
please	*por favór*	excuse me	*perdóneme*
thank you	*gracias*	help!	*ayuda!*
hello	*hola*	today	*hoy*

Best places to see

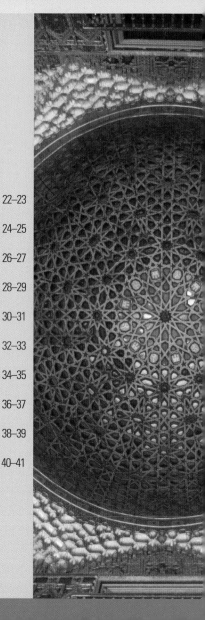

1 La Alhambra, Granada

www.alhambra-patronato.es

La Alhambra is the greatest expression of Moorish culture in Spain, and is one of the world's most spectacular heritage sites.

The Alhambra stands on top of Granada's Sabika Hill, against the background of the often snow-covered massif of the Sierra Nevada. The walled complex is nearly 700m (760 yards) long and about 200m (220 yards) wide. Its name is a corruption of the Arabic *Al Qal'a al-Hamrá*, 'the red castle', a reference to the ruby-red sandstone walls of the Alcazaba, the original fortress built by the 11th-century Emirs of Córdoba.

The Alhambra's other Islamic buildings were constructed during the 13th and 14th centuries by the Nasrids, the last great Moorish rulers, at a time when most of Andalucía, except Granada, had fallen to the 'Reconquest' of Catholic Spain.

There are four groups of buildings: the Alcazaba, on the western escarpment of Sabika; the Casa Real, the 14th-century Royal Palace of the Sultans; the Palace of Carlos V, a 15th-century Renaissance addition; and the Palacio del Generalife, the gardens and summer palace of the Sultans.

The heart of the Alhambra is the Casa Real, which reflects the ingenious manipulation of space and light and of cool water that was the special gift of Moorish architecture. The walls and roofs of its enthralling salons have exquisite stucco work, tiling and decorations that will take your breath away.

🚹 127 E3 ✉ c/ Real s/n ☎ 902 44 12 21 🕐 Mar–Oct daily 8:30–8; floodlit visits Tue–Sat 10pm–11:30pm. Nov–Feb daily 8:30–6; floodlit visits Fri, Sat 8pm–9:30pm ✋ Expensive; free Sun after 3pm. Free daily to visitors with disabilities and senior citizens 🍴 Drinks and snack kiosk 🚌 Alhambrabus every 10 minutes: Plaza Isabel la Católica–Plaza Nueva ❓ Pre-book your Alhambra entry, as numbers are restricted. Tickets can be reserved by phoning 902 22 44 60 (in Spain) or +34 915 37 91 78 (from abroad). You can also book in any BBVA bank branch

2 Las Alpujarras

The southern foothills of the Sierra Nevada, known as Las Alpujarras, were the last stronghold of Moorish influence in medieval Spain.

The hills of Las Alpujarras descend in green waves to the arid river valleys of the Río Guadalfeo in the west and the Río Andarax in the east. On the south side of these valleys lie the Sierra de Contraviesa

and the Sierra de Gádor, mountain barriers that shut out the developed Almerían coast. A more ancient people than the Moors first carved out cultivation terraces and irrigation channels on the hillsides, but the region's history as the final enclave of the Moriscos, nominally Christianized Moors, has given Las Alpujarras much of its romantic appeal.

This is complex and enchanting countryside, which offers superb walking. Driving in Las Alpujarras can also be a pleasure (➤ 76–77), provided you accept that it may take you all day to drive 50km (31 miles) along the great shelf of hills. Narrow, serpentine roads bend to the terraced slopes and sink discreetly into the valleys. Ancient villages and hamlets such as Bayárcal, Yegen and Bérchules invite relaxing halts. The flat-roofed, North African-style houses of the villages are painted white now, but originally the bare stone walls merged with the landscape.

At the heads of the deepest western valleys in the High Alpujarras lie popular villages such as Trevélez, renowned for its *jamón serrano*, the famous cured ham of the mountains. Further west is the Poqueira Gorge, a deep valley striking into the heart of the Sierra Nevada. Clinging to its slopes are the villages of Pampaneira, Bubión and Capileira, from where the wild country of the Sierra is easily reached on foot.

✚ 125 E5 ✉ Southern Sierra Nevada, Granada province

🍴 Bars and restaurants in most villages (€–€€)

🚌 Reguar service Granada–Alpujarra ☎ 958 18 54 80

❓ *Fiesta de San Antonio,* Trevélez, 13–14 Jun; Pilgrimage to the peak of Mulhacén from Trevélez, 5 Aug

3 Gruta de las Maravillas, Aracena

The spectacular limestone formations of Aracena's underground cave system, the Gruta de las Maravillas, are the finest in Andalucía.

Aracena's limestone caves, the Gruta de las Maravillas (Grotto of Marvels, or Cavern of the Wonders) comprise nearly 1.2km (0.75 miles) of illuminated galleries and tunnels that are open to the public. These galleries link 12 spectacular caverns, where limestone deposits have formed stalactites and stalagmites and densely layered flows of calcium carbonate known as tufa. There are six small lakes within the system and the whole is linked by paved walkways, ramps and steps. Carefully arranged lighting adds to the effect and piped music, specially written for the site, murmurs in the background. (Note that the caves can be quite chilly, so take a sweater or jacket.)

Guided tours of the caves are accompanied by commentary in Spanish, but non-Spanish speakers will still enjoy a visually stunning experience. Stay near the back of the crowd and you will have time to admire the fantastic natural architecture that often seems to mirror, with grotesque exaggeration, the intricate decoration of baroque altars and Mudejar façades of Andalucían churches. The caverns all have special names, and the guide points out lifelike figures and faces on the walls and roofs. The final cavern, known famously as the *Sala de los Culos*, the 'Room of the Backsides', is exactly

that: a hilarious extravaganza of comic rude bits, of huge limestone phalluses and tapestries of pink tufa buttocks. You will hear groups of elderly Spanish ladies at the head of the throng shriek with laughter as they reach this part of the tour.

✚ 118 C4 ✉ Pozo de la Nieve s/n ☎ 959 12 82 06
🕐 Daily 10:30–1:30, 3–6. Mon–Fri tours every hour, Sat, Sun tours every half-hour ✋ Moderate 🍴 Casas, Casas Colmenitas 41 (€€) 🚌 Daily Huelva–Aracena, Seville–Aracena ❓ Book tickets at the tourist centre opposite caves' entrance. At busy periods your entry time may be an hour or two after booking

4 Jerez de la Frontera

www.turismojerez.com

Jerez de la Frontera has given its name to sherry, a drink that is popular around the world. It is also a centre of equestrianism and flamenco.

The rich chalky soil of the Jerez area supported vine-growing from the earliest times. Today the coastal region that lies south of a line between Jerez and Sanlúcar de Barrameda is the official sherry-producing area, the Marco de Jerez. The famous sherry-producing bodegas of Jerez are where fermented wine, produced mainly from white Palomino grapes, is stored and transformed into sherry, and where brandy is also produced. Tours of bodegas end with a pleasant tasting session, confirming the precise distinctions between dry *fino* and the darker and sweeter *oloroso* and *amontillado*.

Jerez's other famous institution is the Real Escuela Andaluza del Arte Ecuestre (Royal Andalucían School of Equestrian Art) at Avenida Duque de Abrantes: the horse-riding displays should not be missed. Jerez has excellent cafés, restaurants and shopping, especially in its pedestrian-only main street, Calle Larga. Rewarding visits can be made to the restored 11th-century Alcázar and Arab Baths, the delightful Plaza de la Asunción and the Barrio Santiago, Jerez's old gypsy, or *gitano,* quarter, with its narrow lanes and old churches. In the Barrio you can visit the Museo Arqueológico (Archaeological Museum) in Plaza del Mercado, or see archive material and audio-visual presentations about flamenco at the Centro Andaluz de Flamenco in the Plaza de San Juan.

✚ 122 D1 ✉ 35km (22 miles) northeast of Cádiz, 83km (52 miles) south of Seville 🚉 Plaza de la Estación s/n ☎ 956 34 23 19 🚌 Plaza de la Estación ☎ 956 34 52 07 ❓ *Semana Santa* (Holy Week), Mar/Apr; Horse Fair, early May; *Vendemia*, wine festival, early Sep
ℹ c/ Larga s/n ☎ 956 32 47 47; 956 33 96 28

5 La Mezquita, Córdoba

Of all the Moorish buildings to survive in Andalucía, the Great Mosque of Córdoba is the most haunting and the most Islamic in its forms.

The Mezquita (Mosque) of Córdoba was begun in 785 and expanded and embellished during the following two centuries. You enter the complex by the Patio de los Naranjos, the Courtyard of the Orange Trees, where numerous fountains once

sparkled in the dappled shade and where Muslim worshippers carried out ritual ablutions. The mosque itself is then entered through the modest Puerta de las Palmas. Immediately, you are amid the thickets of columns and arches that are the enduring symbol of the Mezquita. Smooth pillars of marble, jasper and onyx, plundered from the building's Roman and Visigothic predecessors, supplement the total of more than 1,200 columns supporting the horseshoe arches of red brick and white stone. At the far end of the vast interior you will find the *mihrab*, the prayer niche of the mosque, a breathtaking expression of Islamic art.

At the very centre of the Mezquita stands the 1523 Renaissance cathedral of Carlos V, an intrusion that reflected Christian pride rather than piety. Carlos later admitted that the addition of the cathedral had 'destroyed something that was unique in the world'. The cathedral's presence is cloaked by the surrounding pillars of the mosque and made somehow less obvious, although it is the focus of worship today. Its carved mahogany choir stalls are outstanding and there are other striking baroque features, but it is the Islamic Mezquita, with its forest of columns and swirling arches, that is most compelling.

➕ 124 A2 ✉ c/ Torrijos 10 ☎ 957 47 05 12 🕐 Apr–Sep Mon–Sat 10–7, Sun 2–7; Oct–Mar Mon–Sat 10–5, Sun 2–7 ✋ Moderate 🍴 Restaurante Bandolero, c/ Torrijos 6 (€€) 🚌 Avenida de América

6 Parque Natural el Torcal

El Torcal, with its spectacular rock formations, is one of the most remarkable of Andalucía's Natural Parks.

The limestone pinnacles and cliffs of the Sierra del Torcal cover an area of 1,171ha (2,890 acres). The name *Torcal* derives from the word for 'twist' and aptly sums up the maze of narrow, vegetation-filled gullies and ravines among the towering reefs and pillars of rock. From the visitors' car park there are several waymarked circular walking routes through the labyrinth. The shortest route tends to be crowded but there are longer circular routes, and well-worn paths into the labyrinth can be followed, and then retraced. An early-morning or late-afternoon visit is recommended.

The dense undergrowth is formed from holm oak, hawthorn, maple and elder; ivy clings to the rock faces. Flowering plants include saxifrage, peony, rock buttercup, rock rose, thistle and orchid. El Torcal's isolation supports a rich bird life that includes the great grey shrike, vultures and eagles, as well as many small perching birds. There is a good chance of spotting the harmless but fierce-looking ocellated lizard, the largest lizard in Europe.

A short path near the reception centre at the entrance to El Torcal leads to the Mirador de las Ventanillas, a spectacular viewpoint.

✚ 123 D5   ✉ 13km (8 miles) south of Antequera
☎ Reception centre: 952 03 13 89   🕐 Daily 10–5
🍴 Café (€€)

7 Priego de Córdoba

www.turismodepriego.com

The town of Priego de Córdoba is rich in baroque architecture and offers a rare insight into provincial Andalucía.

From Priego's central square, the handsome Plaza de la Constitución, the broad Calle del Río leads southeast past the churches of Our Lady of Anguish and Our Lady of Carmen to a peaceful square with two splendid fountains. These are the

16th-century Fuente del Rey, with its sculpture of Neptune and Amphitrite, and the more restrained Renaissance fountain, the Fuente de la Virgen de la Salud.

From busy Plaza Andalucía, adjoining the Plaza de la Constitución, walk northeast down Solana and through the Plaza San Pedro to a junction with Calle Doctor Pedrajas. To the left is a 16th-century slaughterhouse, the Carnicerías Reales, beautifully preserved with an arcaded patio. Turning right along Calle Doctor Pedrajas brings you to the Plaza Abad Palomina and the privately owned Moorish Castillo. Priego's greatest baroque monument, the Iglesia de la Asunción (Church of the Ascension), is at the far corner of the square. Its plain, whitewashed exterior gives no indication of the treasures inside: a beautifully carved *retablo* (altarpiece) and a spectacular *sagrario* (sacristy), an extravaganza of white stucco, frothing with emblems and statues.

From delightful little Plaza de Santa Ana, alongside the church, head into the Barrio de la Villa down Calle Real, and wander through this old Moorish quarter. Stroll along Calle Jazmines to find the Paseo de Adarve, an airy Moorish promenade with superb views to the surrounding hills.

✚ 124 C3 ✉ 65km (40 miles) southeast of Córdoba
🚌 Regular service Granada–Priego, Córdoba–Priego. Estación de Autobuses, c/ San Marcos
🛈 Carrera de las Monjas 1 ☎ 957 70 06 25 ⏰ Mon–Sat 10–2, 4–7, Sun 10–2

8 Reales Alcázares, Seville

www.patronato-alcazarsevilla.es

The Royal Palaces are a fine example of Mudejar building – Moorish-influenced architecture following the Reconquest.

After Seville fell to Christian forces in 1248, Spanish king Pedro the Cruel reshaped and rebuilt much of the city's original Alcázar in Mudejar style. It is this version that survives at the heart of the present complex, in spite of many restorations and the often clumsy additions made by later monarchs.

Highlights of the Alcázar include the Chapel of the Navigators, where Isabella of Castile masterminded the conquest of the Spanish Americas. The room's coffered wooden ceiling, a classic example of *artesonado* style, is studded with golden stars. Inside the palace proper is the Patio of the Maidens, with fine stucco work and

azulejos tiling. Beyond lies the Salón de Carlos V, with another superb *artesonado* ceiling and then the Alcázar's finest room, the Salon of the Ambassadors, crowned by a glorious dome of wood in green, red and gold and with a Moorish arcade.

Adjoining the main palace are the dull and cavernous chambers of the Palacio de Carlos V, added by that insatiable intruder upon fine buildings, the Hapsburg king. These lead to the serene and lovely gardens of the Alcázar, where an arc of water from a high faucet crashes spectacularly into a pool in which a bronze statue of Mercury stands in front of a rusticated façade: the Gallery of the Grotesque. The rest of the gardens are a pleasant conclusion before you emerge into the Patio de las Banderas, with Seville's mighty cathedral beckoning ahead.

✚ 127 B2 ✉ Patio de las Banderas ☎ 954 50 23 23 🕐 Oct–Mar Tue–Sat 9:30–5, Sun 9:30–1:30; Apr–Oct Tue–Sat 9:30–7, Sun 9:30–5 ✋ Moderate; children under 12 and senior citizens free 🚌 C1, C2, C3, C4 ❓ A visit early or late in the day may win you some added space. At busier times, numbers are regulated and you may have to wait your turn
ℹ Avenida de la Constitución 21B
☎ 954 22 14 04; 954 21 81 57

9 Úbeda

Although famous for its Moorish architecture, Andalucía is also home to some of Spain's finest Renaissance buildings. Úbeda has some of the best.

Renaissance Úbeda survives triumphantly within its more modern and often featureless surroundings. To reach the crowning glory of the Plaza de Vázquez de Molina you need to navigate the urban maze from the town's modern centre at the busy Plaza de Andalucía. From here the narrow Calle Real runs gently downhill to the Plaza del Ayuntamiento, where a short street leads to the glorious enclave of Plaza de Vázquez de Molina. Just before entering the plaza, you will find, on the right, Úbeda's remarkable Museo de Alfarería (Pottery Museum).

On the right as you enter Plaza de Vázquez de Molina is the Palacio de las Cadenas, the work of the great classical architect Andrés Vandelvira. Directly opposite is the handsome Church of Santa María de los Reales Alcázares, enclosing a lovely Gothic cloister on the site of an original Moorish building. East of here lie other fine buildings, culminating in a 16th-century palace, now Úbeda's luxurious Parador hotel.

At the east end of the plaza is the Sacra Capilla del Salvador. This private burial chapel dates from the mid-16th century and was completed by Vandelvira to an earlier design. The grand exterior

apart, inside you will find a carefully restored *retablo* (altarpiece) of breathtaking splendour, beneath a soaring cupola. Other fine buildings and churches are found in Plaza San Pedro, reached from halfway down Calle Real, and in Plaza del Primero de Mayo, just north of Plaza de Vázquez de Molina.

➕ 125 B5 ✉ 45km (28 miles) northeast of Jaén
🚌 Regular service Jaén–Úbeda, Granada–Úbeda, Baeza–Úbeda ❓ *Fiesta de San Miguel*, 4 Oct
ℹ Palacio del Marqués del Contadero, c/ Bajo del Marqués 4 ☎ 953 75 08 97

10 Zahara de la Sierra

Hailed as one of the finest of the *pueblos blancos* ('white towns') of Ronda, Zahara de la Sierra occupies a spectacular hilltop position, offering wonderful views.

The red-roofed, white-walled houses of the lovely village of Zahara cluster beneath a dramatic hilltop castle at the heart of the Sierra Margarita in the Parque Natural Sierra de Grazalema. Below, to the northeast, is a large reservoir, the Embalse de Zahara, formed by damming the Río Guadalete. Zahara's castle has Roman origins but was rebuilt by the Moors during the 12th century. It was later occupied by Christians, and its reckless retaking by the forces of Granada's Nasrid rulers in 1481 prompted Ferdinand and Isabella to launch the final conquest of Moorish Granada and its province.

If you visit Zahara by car, it is best to find a roadside parking space near the top of the steep approach road before entering the centre of the village. Zahara is a delightful hilltop enclave, its Moorish character intact. The renovated castle is reached from the village square by following a winding pathway uphill past a charming cave fountain. The views from the castle and its tower are spectacular, but take care on the steep, unlit steps. The tiny village square stands in front of the baroque church of Santa María de la

Mesa and there is an airy *mirador*, a viewing balcony, overlooking the reservoir. At the other end of the main street, at the entrance to the village, is the little church of San Juan, which houses some vivid statues. At night Zahara's castle is floodlit and its centre and side streets take on an engaging intimacy.

➕ 122 D3 ✉ 22km (14 miles) northwest of Ronda

🚌 Regular service Ronda–Zahara de la Sierra

❓ *Corpus Christi,* end May–early Jun

ℹ Plaza de la Rey 3 ☎ 956 12 31 14

Exploring

Sunseeker, sightseer, foodie: whatever you love, Andalucía will get your heart racing. It's a thrillingly varied, beautiful region of Spain, drenched in sunlight for most of the year. Yes, parts have become stale with resort developments, but that's all the more reason to explore the enthralling interior, where you'll receive a warm welcome, and perhaps a chilled glass of *fino*.

The Moors conquered this southern area of Spain, which extends from the pounding surf of the Atlantic to the green rolling hills of Jerez, eastward to the mountains of the Sierra Nevada, in a couple of centuries. They left their mark in a series of buildings – from Granada's Alhambra to Córdoba's Mezquita – that are wonders of the Islamic world. Andalucían cities are among Spain's most vibrant, with Seville and Córdoba leading the nation in flamenco and tapas. Cádiz has an air of faded glamour, while Jerez is famous for sherry.

Córdoba and Jaén Provinces

The provinces of Córdoba and Jaén are where Moorish and Renaissance Spain overlap and where a more northern European influence has imposed itself on Mediterranean Andalucía.

□ Córdoba

□ Jaén

The Río (river) Guadalquivir neatly divides Córdoba province, and the city of Córdoba stands on its northern banks. To the north and

west lie the smooth, wooded hills of the Sierra Morena; south is the farming country of the Campiña, dotted with olives and vines and patched with fields of golden grain. Here lie delightful towns and villages such as Priego de Córdoba and Zuheros.

The city of Jaén and the nearby towns of Baeza and Úbeda are more Renaissance than Moorish. They sit at the centre of Jaén province, a landscape of regimented olive trees (these have provided Jaén's staple product for centuries), where low hills extend towards the dramatic mountain wall of the Sierra Cazorla in the east.

CÓRDOBA

The city of Córdoba has a spectacular past. In 152BC the Romans founded their settlement of *Corduba* on the banks of the Río Guadalquivir, and for six centuries the city flourished, enriched by trade in olive oil, minerals and wool. Moorish conquest in the 8th century eventually made Córdoba a glittering rival to Baghdad as a centre of Islamic culture.

Modern Córdoba is a small city with a big heart. It has an engaging intimacy not found in Granada or Seville and is less traffic-bound than these main urban centres. The pedestrian-only central areas merge satisfyingly with the narrow streets of the Judería, the old quarter that encloses the Mezquita (➤ 30–31), Córdoba's world-renowned mosque, a breathtaking survivor of Moorish Andalucía. In hidden corners of the city, away from the crowded areas, you will feel the engaging spirit of an older Spain.

A visit to the ruins of the 10th-century palace of **Medina Azahara,** a few kilometres outside the city, gives some perspective on Córdoba's importance during the Moorish period. In the 11th century the Christian Reconquest signalled the beginning of the city's decline, until 20th-century agriculture, light industry and tourism shaped the flourishing Córdoba of today.

This city has great style, which is reflected in its mix of lively bars and top-quality restaurants, and in its fashionable shops. The happy merging of the past with the present is what makes Córdoba so appealing.

➕ 124 A2 🚹 c/ Torrijos 10 ☎ 957 47 12 35
❓ *Fiesta de los Patios*, early May

Medina Azahara

✉ 7km (4 miles) west of Córdoba, on the CP199 off the A431 ☎ 957 32 91 30
🕐 Tue–Sat and Sun mornings 🚻 Inexpensive; free with EU passport

Alcázar de los Reyes Cristianos

Córdoba's Alcázar de los Reyes Cristianos (Palace of the Christian Kings) is an interesting hybrid of Christian and Moorish features that epitomize the Mudejar architectural styles of medieval Andalucía. It was built during the late 13th century, soon after the Reconquest, as a palace for the Christian monarchs. The building houses a museum in which there are some outstanding Roman mosaics. The sunny gardens are ablaze with colourful flowers and shrubs, while ponds and fountains glitter in the unforgiving sunlight. Cool interiors compensate for the heat.

✉ Plaza Campo Santo de los Mártires ☎ 957 42 01 51 🕐 Tue–Sat 10–2, 4:30–7:30, Sun 9:30–2:30 ✋ Moderate; free Tue 🍴 Bar-Restaurante Millán, Avenida Dr Fleming 14 (€€)

Judería

The engaging maze of narrow alleys that lies between the Plaza Tendillas and the Mezquita is the Judería, Córdoba's old Jewish quarter. The area of the Judería close to the Mezquita is given over to souvenir shops, but there is still much charm in popular venues such as the flower-bedecked Callejón de las Flores, a narrow cul-de-sac whose walls neatly frame the Mezquita's old minaret tower. At Calle Maimónides 18, near the Museum of Bullfighting, there is a 14th-century synagogue, the only one in Andalucía and a good example of Mudejar architecture. Near the synagogue is the Puerta de Almodóvar, a 14th-century city gate flanked by a statue of the Roman scholar Seneca, who was born in the Judería.

La Mezquita

Best places to see, ➤ 30–31.

Museo Arqueológico Provincial

Córdoba's Archaeological Museum occupies a delightful Renaissance mansion, the Palacio de los Páez. The arcaded entrance patio (a well-known Córdoban feature), along with the building's coffered ceilings and elegant staircases, enhances the excellent displays of prehistoric, Roman and Moorish exhibits. These include Roman mosaics and tombstones, and a Moorish bronze in the form of a stag, found at the ruins of Medina Azahara (➤ 46).

✉ Plaza Jerónimo Páez ☎ 957 35 55 17 🕐 Tue 2:30–8:30, Wed–Sat 9–8:30, Sun 9–2:30 ✋ Inexpensive; free with EU passport
🍴 Several cafés (€–€€€)

49

More to see in Córdoba and Jaén Provinces

BAEZA

Renaissance elegance is the hallmark of Baeza's old quarter, where remnants of long years of Moorish influence have been replaced with 16th-century classical buildings of the highest order. The busy, central Plaza de España extends into the tree-lined Paseo de la Constitución, with its lively pavement bars and cafés. The town's Renaissance treasures lie on the higher ground, east of here. At the southern end of the Paseo de la Constitución is the handsome Plaza de los Leones, also known as Plaza del Pópulo, with its fountain and double-arched gateway, the Puerta de Jaén.

Steps (Escalerillas de la Audienca) lead from the tourist office, then left to Plaza Santa Cruz, where you will find the Palace of Jabalquinto, with its superbly ornamented Gothic façade. The Renaissance courtyard and glorious baroque staircase are in poor condition, but are being refurbished. Opposite the palace is the

delightful little Romanesque church of Santa Cruz, with traces of the earlier mosque that it supplanted.

Cuesta de San Felipe leads uphill from Plaza Santa Cruz to Plaza de Santa María, the heart of Renaissance Baeza. The plaza is dominated by Baeza's 13th-century cathedral, which has a superb 16th-century nave. At the square's centre is a fountain in the form of a rustic triumphal arch, behind which stands the 16th-century seminary of San Felipe Neri, its walls bearing elegant graffiti.

🚹 125 B5 ✉ 48km (30 miles) northeast of Jaén 🚌 Regular services Jaén–Baeza, Granada–Baeza, Úbeda–Baeza 🚆 Railway station at Linares-Baeza, 14km (9 miles) from Baeza; connecting buses

❓ *Semana Santa* (Holy Week), Mar/Apr; *Romería del Cristo de la Yedra*, 7 Sep

ℹ️ Plaza del Pópulo s/n ☎ 953 74 04 44

BAÑOS DE LA ENCINA

This engaging hilltop village rises from acres of olive fields. It is dominated by its well-preserved, 10th-century Moorish castle. The custodian may be at the airy *mirador* on the way up to the castle; if not, ask at the Town Hall. You will be ushered through the double horseshoe arch into a huge central keep, where you can climb the Tower of Homage. Take care on the dark stairways: pigeons often explode into the light, and you may find their eggs perched mid-step. The views from the top are magnificent. Resist the challenge to walk round the inner, unprotected parapet if you do not have good footwork.

🚹 125 A5 ✉ 100km (62 miles) east of Córdoba 🚌 Regular services Córdoba–Bailén, Úbeda–Bailén; local bus connections between Bailén and Baños

ℹ️ Avenida José Luís Messias 2 ☎ 953 613 266

CAZORLA

The busy, unpretentious town of Cazorla nestles below the looming cliffs of the Peña de los Halcones. There is a lively daily market in Plaza del Mercado between the car park and Calle Dr Muñoz, the main shopping street. Plaza de la Corredera, Cazorla's more sedate square, is surrounded by cafés and shops. From its far right-hand corner the narrow Calle Nubla leads past the superb Balcón del Pintor Zabaleta, for views of Cazorla's ruined Moorish castle, La Yedra, and its ruined Renaissance church of Santa María. Ruination apart, Plaza Santa María, below the church, is a wonderful place to eat and drink.

The town is gateway to the Parque Natural de Cazorla, Segura y Las Villas, a marvellous area of mountains and forests, where the Guadalquivir river has its source (► 56).

✚ 125 B6 ✉ 32km (20 miles) southeast of Úbeda 🚌 Regular services Granada–Cazorla, Jaén–Cazorla, Úbeda–Cazorla ❓ Pilgrimage to La Virgen de la Cabeza, last Sun/Mon in Apr

ℹ Paseo del Santo Cristo 17 ☎ 953 71 01 02; c/ Hilario Marco; Parque Natural Information Centre, c/ Martínez Falero 11 ☎ 953 71 15 34

JAÉN

Jaén is often given short shrift in terms of its appeal to the visitor. It is a pleasant enough city, however, though not as exotically Andalucían as other centres. Moorish moods still prevail in the old quarters of La Magdalena and San Juan, on the northeastern slopes of the Hill of Santa Catalina, and exploration of their streets is rewarding.

The scrub-covered Hill of Santa Catalina is crowned by the Castillo de Santa Catalina, its remnants transformed into a

luxurious *parador* (state-run hotel). It is a stiff hike to the top of the hill, but the view from the cross-crowned *mirador* near the southern ruins is spectacular.

Down at street level, Jaén's main attraction is its vast and magnificent 16th-century cathedral. The west façade is a fine example of Renaissance baroque. The gloomy interior has an impressive display of fluted Corinthian columns and rich carving. Other fine sights in Jaén include the Baños Árabes (Arab Baths), in the basement of the arts and crafts museum at the 16th-century Palacio de Villadompardo, just off Plaza San Blas. Another worthwhile visit can be made to the Museo Provincial in Paseo de la Estación. Collections from prehistory to Moorish and Renaissance times vie with the Museo de Bellas Artes (Museum of Fine Arts) upstairs, where there are some spectacularly bad but entertaining paintings, with provocative nudes in abundance.

www.andalucia.org

🔳 124 B4 ✉ 90km (56 miles) east of Córdoba

🚊 Paseo de la Estación ☎ 902 24 02 02

🚌 Plaza Coca de la Piñera ☎ 953 25 01 06

❓ *Semana Santa* (Holy Week), Mar/Apr; *Feria de San Lucas,* mid-Oct

ℹ c/ de la Maestra 13 ☎ 953 31 32 81

PRIEGO DE CÓRDOBA

Best places to see, ➤ 34–35.

a drive through the Sierras

This is quite a long drive, with a great deal to see. An overnight stop at somewhere like Segura de la Sierra is worthwhile.

From Úbeda go east along the N322, signed Valencia, Albacete. After 2km (1.25 miles), bear right, signed Cazorla. Watch carefully for a 'Halt' sign and at a roundabout, take the exit signed A315, Cazorla.

The road winds pleasantly towards distant mountains through low hills covered with olive trees. Fields of wheat and barley shine like gold in early summer.

At the main square of Cazorla (▶ 52) go round the roundabout and take the higher road marked 'Sierra' on its surface and signed for Parque Natural. Pass La Iruela village, where a ruined castle stands on a rock pinnacle. At Burunchal take the right fork, signed Parque Natural. Follow the winding A319 through magnificent scenery. After 15km (9 miles), go left at a junction signed Coto Ríos (or for a walk, ▶ 58–59).

The road follows the Guadalquivir valley through beautiful wooded mountains, passes the visitors' centre at Torre del Vinagre, then runs alongside the Tranco reservoir.

Two thirds of the way along the reservoir, cross a dam and keep right at the junction. After 9km (5.5 miles), at a junction below the hilltop village of Hornos, go left, signed

Cortijos Nuevos. Go through Cortijos and at the roundabout take the second right, signed La Puerta de Segura. Continue on the A317 and follow signs for Puerta de Segura and Albacete. Drive carefully through Puerta de Segura, then follow signs for Puente Génave and Úbeda. Join the N322 and return to Úbeda.

Distance 214km (133 miles)
Time 8 hours
Start/End point Úbeda ✚ 125 B5
Lunch Café de la Corredera (€) ✉ Plaza de la Corredera, Cazorla

SIERRAS DE CAZORLA, SEGURA Y LAS VILLAS

The Sierras of Cazorla, Segura and Las Villas make up the largest of Andalucía's Parque Naturales (Natural Parks) at an impressive 214,000ha (530,000 acres). The Sierras are a complex of deep valleys and high ridges, with the mountain of Las Empanadas being the highest point at 2,107m (6,910ft). This is a winter landscape of snow and ice, but in late spring, summer and autumn the Sierras are delightful, often hot and sunny, yet verdant, with higher than average rainfall for such terrain. There are good opportunities for short or long walks, and you can also book trips on off-road Land Rovers. More than 1,000 plant species include the Cazorla violet, unique to the area. Trees include the black pine, Aleppo pine and evergreen oaks, and there is a multitude of animals large and small, including fox, wild cat, polecat, otter, deer, mountain goat and wild boar. Birds include griffon vulture, booted and golden eagles, peregrine falcon and kite.

At Torre del Vinagre, 34km (21 miles) northeast of Cazorla, there is an **interpretation centre**, where you can book Land Rover trips and mountain bike or horse rides.

✚ 125 B6/B7 ✉ 90km (56 miles) northeast of Jaén ⍢ Bars, cafés and restaurants (€–€€) 🚌 Twice daily Cazorla–Torre del Vinagre–Cotos Ríos ℹ Parque Natural Information Centre, c/ Martinez Falero 11, Cazorla ☎ 953 71 15 34

Centro de Interpretación Torre del Vinagre

✉ Torre del Vinagre ☎ 953 71 30 17 🕐 Summer daily 10–2, 5–8:30; spring and autumn daily 11–2, 4–7:30; winter Tue–Sun 11–2, 4–5:30

SEGURA DE LA SIERRA

It is a challenging, tortuous drive to reach this village, which perches on a 1,100m (3,600ft) hill surrounded by peaks. You enter the village through a medieval gateway. Below the tiny Plaza de la Encomienda is the Iglesia Nuestra Señora del Collado, a handsome church with tiled roof and simple interior. Opposite the church is a

Renaissance fountain, the Fuente Carlos V. Near the church is a well-preserved Arab bath house.

Segura's castle has been much renovated over the years. You may need to ask for the key at the tourist office, but the gate is often open – a reward for the stiff climb past the Plaza de Toros, Segura's tiny bullring. During the October festival there is a *corrida* (bullfight) here; famous matadors, such as Enrique Ponce, have fought here. The view from the castle tower is outstanding, but take care on the dark stairways.

➕ 125 A7 ✉ 60km (37 miles) northeast of Úbeda 🍴 Casa Mesón Jorge Manríque (€€) 🛈 *Santa Quiteria*, 22 May; *Santiago*, 25 Jul; *Virgen del Rosario*, 5–8 Oct 🛈 c/ Regidor Juan de Isla, 1 ☎ 953 48 07 84

ÚBEDA
Best places to see, ➤ 38–39.

ZUHEROS
The white houses of Zuheros cluster below a Moorish castle in the Sierra Subbética, in a world of cliffs and rocky bluffs. The village has a handsome church, the Iglesia de la Virgen de los Remedios, whose tower supplanted an earlier minaret. The narrow streets are punctuated by fine viewpoints such as the Mirador de la Villa. East of Zuheros is the Cueva de los Murciélagos (Cave of the Bats), with prehistoric paintings (with guided tours at weekends).

➕ 124 B3 ✉ 60km (37 miles) southeast of Córdoba 🍴 Mesón Atalaya, c/ Santo 58 (€) 🛈 Plaza de le Paz 2 ☎ 957 69 45 45

a walk along the Guadalquivir

A short walk through dramatic mountain scenery alongside the infant Río Guadalquivir.

From the parking space, walk downhill to reach a bridge over the Río Guadalquivir. Don't cross the bridge but turn left along a rocky path.

The Guadalquivir was named Guad al Quivir (Great River) by the Moors. It rises in the heart of the Sierra Cazorla and flows through Andalucía for 657km (407 miles) to the sea at Sanlúcar de Barrameda.

Follow the rocky path as it rises along the side of the river valley. Descend steeply and go down winding steps to reach a weir. Go down steps to the base of a waterfall that drops from the weir.

The valley widens here and is flanked by great cliffs. Dragonflies and damselflies flit across the river pools.

Continue along the path beneath overhanging cliffs. There are shaded seats alongside the path.

Swifts dip and weave through the sky from their nests in the looming rocks above. Keep an eye open for mountain goats, which often graze at these lower levels.

Soon the path leads above a deep wooded valley and reaches a superb viewpoint just beyond an old well head and water pipe. Continue along a track through trees and keep left on the main track. At the next junction go right to reach a road and large parking area beside a notice board. Turn left and go downhill for a short distance to the parking space.

Distance 2km (1.25 miles)
Time 1 hour
Start/end point Follow instructions for the Sierras drive (► 54–55) to the turning at the junction signed Coto Ríos; keep right here, signed Parador de Turismo. There's a café and seating at the base of the hill. The road worsens here noticeably. At the next junction keep left, signed Vadillo Castril. Soon, at a wide area, reach a junction with a road bending sharply right. Keep ahead for about 100m (110 yards) to a parking space on the right, just before a small house ✚ 124 D1
Lunch Parador de Cazorla (€€€) ✉ Sierra de Cazorla s/n ☎ 953 72 70 75

Granada and Almería Provinces

Granada

Almería

The provinces of Granada and Almería contain Andalucía's most diverse landscapes. Granada province has the great mountain range of the Sierra Nevada at its heart, where the snow-streaked summit of Mulhacén rises above the foothills of Las Alpujarras. Further east into Almería province, the green dwindles into an increasingly parched landscape of brown and ochre hills.

Both provinces border the Mediterranean, where the holiday areas of the Costa de Almería and the Costa Tropical add to the provinces' diversity. The city of Granada is famous for the spectacular Alhambra, one of the world's great architectural treasures, and Almería city boasts its own fortified Moorish palace, the Alcázaba.

The fascinating diversity of the two provinces extends to the towns and villages of the coast and interior, from the beach resort of Mójacar to the mountain villages of Trevélez and Capileira, and from the pottery villages of Níjar and Sorbas to the cave dwellings of Guadix.

GRANADA

Granada stands at the foot of the Sierra Nevada massif, which acts as its dramatic backdrop. Dominating the town is the Alhambra (► 22–23), perched on its hilltop site facing the high ground of the Moorish quarter of Albaicín across the valley of the Río Darro. The Alhambra apart, there is much to see in Granada, from the stately cathedral to the remarkable buildings of the university quarter, and from the fashionable streets of the modern city to the bazaar-like alleyways linking the old city's delightful plazas.

Granada was the last stronghold of the Moors, the final jewel in the crown of the 15th-century Catholic Reconquest of Andalucía. From the early 8th century, the city was controlled from Moorish Córdoba, and then from Seville. In the 1240s Granada emerged as the capital of a separate and successful kingdom under the rule of an independent Arab prince of the Nasrid dynasty. Moorish Granada and its province survived intact for another two centuries until its final conquest in 1492 by Ferdinand and Isabella. Jealous of Moorish grandeur, they set a northern Spanish stamp on Granada, yet preserved the mighty Alhambra, the most spectacular of Andalucía's surviving Moorish monuments.
www.turgranada.es

✚ 124 D4 🛈 Plaza de Mariana Pineda 10–2 ☎ 958 24 71 28
🕔 Mon–Fri 9–8, Sat 10–7, Sun 10–3

The Albaicín

Granada's antidote to its modern city streets is the engaging Albaicín, the old Moorish quarter that occupies the northern side of the valley of the Río Darro and the hill of Sacromonte, the city's much vaunted *gitano*, or gypsy, quarter. The Albaicín is best reached from Plaza Nueva by following the Carrera del Darro, past the Baños Árabes (► 64) and the Museo Arqueológico (► 67) and on beyond the attractive terrace of

Paseo de los Tristes, where there are numerous cafés in the shade of the Alhambra Hill. You can plunge into the heart of the Albaicín by going along the Carrera del Darro and its continuation of Paseo del Padre Manjón, and then by turning left up Cuesta del Chapiz. Part of the way up, the Camino del Sacromonte leads off right into the gypsy quarter and the notorious 'flamenco caves', where you risk off-loading large sums of money to watch insistent but not entirely authentic flamenco shows.

The real pleasures of the Albaicín lie in the maze of streets and marvellous local plazas, with their bars and restaurants. Find your way to the famous Mirador de San Nicolás for a world-famous sunset view of the Alhambra; but hang on to your bag, *very tightly*; the local thieves are absolute masters at spiriting away anything moveable the minute it is put down.

✚ 127 E3 ✉ Northeast of Plaza Nueva 🍴 Numerous bars and restaurants (€–€€) 🚌 Alhambrabus

Baños Árabes

On the way along the Carrera del Darro from Plaza Nueva are the Baños Árabes (Arab Baths), a small but enchanting Moorish bathhouse, entered through a tiny courtyard garden with an inlaid floor and tiny central pool. The 11th-century baths are well-preserved and have the typical star-shape and octagon-shape skylights in the roofs of their brick-vaulted chambers.

🕇 127 E3 ⊠ Carrera del Darro 31 ☎ 958 02 78 00 ⏱ Tue–Sat 10–2
✋ Free 🍴 Several in Paseo de los Tristes (€–€€) 🚌 Alhambrabus

Capilla Real

The Capilla Real (Royal Chapel) was built between 1506 and 1521 as a sepulchre for Los Reyes Católicos, Ferdinand and Isabella, one of the most terrifying double acts in history. The Royal Chapel is an

intriguing Gothic building, an odd mixture of the flamboyant and the restrained. It is impressive, yet lacks entirely the subtle elegance of Moorish buildings. Inside lies the Renaissance monument in Carrera marble celebrating the two monarchs. Note how the head of Isabella's effigy is more deeply sunk into her pillow than Ferdinand's – a reflection, it is said, of her undoubtedly superior intelligence. Below the monument, down narrow steps, lie the lead coffins of the monarchs, their daughter Joana and her husband Felipe, although there is no certainty that they contain the genuine remains of anyone.

The most striking feature of the chapel is the altar's superb *retablo* (alterpiece), a gilded extravaganza. In the sacristy are displayed, among royal heirlooms, Isabella's splendid collection of paintings by Flemish masters and others.

✚ 127 F2 ✉ Oficios 3 ☎ 958 22 92 39 ◷ Apr–Oct Mon–Sat 10:30–1, 4–7, Sun 11–1, 4–7; Nov–Mar Mon–Sat 10:30–1, 3:30–6:30, Sun 11–1, 3:30–6:30 ✋ Inexpensive 🍴 Bar-Restaurante Sevilla, c/ Oficios 12 (€€) 🚌 1, 3, 4, 6, 7, 8, 9

Catedral

Granada's cathedral stands near the apex of the busy junction of Gran Vía de Colón and Calle Reyes Católicos. The cathedral is crowded round by other buildings, but its massiveness and its stepped exterior of tiled turrets, gables and buttresses rising to a central dome dominate the cramped surroundings. The building dates from the 16th century and reflects all the contemporary certainties that raised it in place of a demolished mosque. The high central dome, supported on huge pillars, lends lightness to the interior and to the wealth of baroque chapels.

✚ 127 F2 ✉ Gran Vía de Colón 5 ☎ 958 22 29 59 ◷ Mon–Sat 10:45–1:30, 4–8, Sun and public hols 4–8 (7 in winter) ✋ Inexpensive 🍴 Vía Colona, Gran Vía de Colón 13 (€€) 🚌 1, 3, 4, 6, 7, 8, 9

Monasterio de la Cartuja

The Monasterio de la Cartuja (Monastery of the Carthusians) lies some way from the city centre, but it is well worth the journey. This is the most extravagant of Spain's Carthusian buildings and dates from the early 16th century. The Cartuja's monastery and church face each other across an attractive patio, but it is the church that is the real showstopper – it's a lavish torrent of baroque sculpture, all swirling marble and jasper and gilded frescoes.

✚ 127 D1 *(off map)* ✉ c/ Real de Cartuja ☎ 958 16 19 32 ◑ Mon–Sun 10–1, 4–8 ✋ Inexpensive 🚌 8 C

Monasterio de San Jerónimo

The 16th-century Monasterio de San Jerónimo (Monastery of St Jeronimo) lies in the university district to the northwest of the cathedral. Its focus is a central patio, a superb example of mixed Gothic-Renaissance features and with refreshingly peaceful cloisters, where the mellow chanting of the nuns at prayer can often be heard. The adjoining church has an inspiring interior, all painted frescoes and with a glorious four-storeyed *retablo* (altarpiece) within an octagonal apse.

The adjacent university district has a wealth of remarkable churches and secular buildings to offset the lively bustle of student life.

🗺 127 E1 *(off map)* ✉ Rector López Argueta 9 ☎ 958 27 93 37 🕒 Mon–Sun 10–2:30, 4–7:30 🖐 Inexpensive 🍴 Numerous cafés in adjoining San Juan de Dios (€) 🚌 5

Museo Arqueológico

The Museo Arqueológico (Archaeological Museum) lies within a delightful Renaissance palace – the Casa de Castril. The building has a central patio from whose upper balcony you can see the Alhambra across a frieze of tiled roofs. Exhibited in these elegant surroundings are artefacts from the prehistoric, Phoenician, Roman, Visigothic and Moorish periods.

www.junta-andalucia.es/cultura

🗺 127 E3 ✉ Carrera del Darro 43 ☎ 958 22 56 40 🕒 Wed–Sat 9–8, Sun 9–2:30, Tue 3–8. Closed Mon 🖐 Inexpensive; free with EU passport 🚌 Alhambrabus, 31, 32

a walk in Granada's Albaicín

From Plaza Nueva walk through Plaza Santa Ana past the Iglesia de Santa Ana y San Gil, and along the narrow Carrera del Darro, keeping a lookout for traffic.

You pass the old Moorish bridge, the Puente de Cabrera, and then the Puente de Espinosa. From here you can see the walls of the Alhambra looming high above.

Continue along Carrera del Darro, passing the Convento de Santa Catalina de Zafra and the Museo Arqueológico on your left. Keep on past the terrace of Paseo del Padre Manjón. After Café Bar La Fuente, turn left up narrow, pebbled Calle Horno del Oro. Go up steps at the top of the alley, then turn right up some more steps. Cross a

lane and continue up pebbled Calle Valenzuela. At its top go up more steps, bear left, then turn right at a junction. In 20m (22 yards) go sharply left, then uphill and round to the right. At a junction with Carril de San Agustín, go sharply left and up the pebbled lane. Follow the lane round to the right and keep on, past a junction on the left.

You'll pass the Aljibe de Bibalbonud, a brick-built Moorish well, and Convento Santo Tomás de Villanueva.

Continue through the tree-lined Placeta del Abad and go alongside the wall of the church of San Salvador. Turn left to reach the entrance to the church.

The church was built on the site of a 13th-century mosque, and the original patio still survives.

Turn left, and then left again into Calle Panaderos. Pass another old well, the Aljibe de Polo, and continue past small shops and bars to reach tree-shaded Plaza Larga. Cross the plaza to its opposite corner and go under the Puerta de la Pesas (Gate of the Weights), a gateway in the old walls of the Albaicín's original Moorish castle. Beyond the arch, climb steps into Placeta de las Minas, turn left along Callejón San Cecilio and follow the lane round right to reach Plaza del Cementerio de San Nicolás.

To the right of the 16th-century church is a Moorish cistern, still spouting water. Immediately in front of the church is the Mirador de San Nicolás, Granada's most famous viewpoint. Keep a strong grip on your belongings here.

Go down the right-hand side of the Mirador, keep downhill, then go right along Nuevo de San Nicolás. At a crossing, turn left onto narrow Cuesta María de la Miel, then at a T-junction turn right along Algibe del Gato. In a few metres, go down left and then round right and into Placeta Nevot. Keep going downhill and on through Placeta de la Cruz Verde. Continue down San Gregorio, then along Calderería Nueva passing Granada's fast-growing modern "Arab quarter". Reach a T-junction with Calle de Elvira, and turn left to return to Plaza Nueva.

Distance 3km (2 miles)
Time 2–3 hours
Start/end point Plaza Nueva ✚ 127 E3

More to see in Granada and Almería Provinces

ALHAMA DE GRANADA

Alhama, on the lip of a rocky gorge, was a significant Moorish settlement due to its hot springs, *al hamma*. These still attract devotees to the nearby hotel Balneario. The town's main square, the Plaza de la Constitución, is a pleasant place in which to enjoy good tapas at surrounding bars. The Moorish castle at the end of the lower square is privately owned. Nearby is the Iglesia del Carmen, a handsome late-medieval church with a lovely stone fountain outside. On the far side of the Iglesia del Carmen is a terrace overlooking the gorge of the Río Alhama. From the fountain in front of the church, walk with the gorge on your right, to Calle Portillo Naveros, then go left up Calle Baja Iglesia. Pass the charming Casa de la Inquisición, a small building with a perfect façade in the late Gothic/early Renaissance Plateresque style. Then reach the pleasing little square Plaza los Presos and the handsome 16th-century Renaissance church of La Encarnación.

⊕ 124 D3 ✉ 40km (26 miles) southwest of Granada 🍴 Café-Bar Andaluz, Plaza de la Constitución (€) 🚌 Mon–Fri Granada–Alhama de Granada
ℹ c/ Vendederas ☎ 958 36 06 86

ALMERÍA

Almería was one of the great cities of Moorish Andalucía, rivalling Seville, but after the Reconquest, the Spanish rulers neglected the port, and a series of earthquakes during the 16th century ruined large parts of the city. Today, Almería has great appeal as an essentially Spanish city with a distinctive North African flavour. Its most enduring monument is the Moorish Alcazaba.

Modern Almería is divided into east and west by the Rambla de Belén, a wide boulevard that has replaced an unsightly dry river bed. West of the Rambla is the Paseo de Almería. Halfway down the Paseo, a broad alley leads to Almería's colourful morning market. At the north end of Paseo de Almería is Puerta de

Purchena, the city's real focus, a busy junction groaning with traffic, but also bustling with life. Calle de las Tiendas, running south from Puerta de Purchena, is one of Almería's oldest streets, now a fashionable shopping venue. Attractive side streets lead via Plaza Flores and Torres Siloy to the Plaza San Pedro, with its handsome church and raised promenade.

Just west of Plaza San Pedro is the Plaza Vieja (Old Square), also known as the Plaza de la Constitución. This 17th-century arcaded square, a northern Spanish interloper to Moorish Almería, is entered through narrow alleyways. The central space is occupied by palm trees and a bone-white monument. On the west side is the theatrical façade of the Ayuntamiento (Town Hall).

www.andalucia.org

✠ 125 F7

ℹ Parque San Nicolás Salmerón ☎ 950 27 43 55

La Alcazaba de Almería

La Alcazaba dominates Almería, although the modern town seems oddly detached from it. The happily scruffy Barrio de Chanca, a district of brightly painted, flat-roofed houses, surges up to its walls. An entrance ramp winds steeply up to Puerta de la Justicia (the Justice Gate), unmistakably Moorish in style. Beyond is the First Precinct, cleverly renovated and reflecting, in its gardens and water channels, what the original must have been like. The views

over the city are superb. A gentle climb past flowering shrubs and tinkling water leads to a beautiful oasis of trees hard against the walls of the Second Precinct. Here marble slabs, inscribed with verses by García Lorca and Fernando Villalón, rest against the wall. Inside the Second Precinct are the foundations of Moorish bathhouses. The Third Precinct encloses the triangular fortress, originally Moorish but greatly strengthened by the Christians. The views are breathtaking. Across the broad valley of San Cristóbal to the west is the Mirador de San Cristóbal, linked to the Alcazaba by the Muralla de San Cristóbal, a distinctive fortified wall.

✉ Almanzor s/n ☎ 950 17 55 00 🕐 Nov–Apr daily 9–6:30; Apr–Nov 9–8:30 💶 Inexpensive; free with EU passport 🍴 Bar/café (€€)

Catedral

Almería's cathedral seems more fortress than church. Its stark and formidable walls were built to repel the pirates and disaffected Moriscos who haunted the coast in the aftermath of the Christian Reconquest. Look for the cheerful yet unexplained sun symbol on the east wall, at the entrance to the pleasing little Plaza Bendicho. The interior is fiercely Gothic and dark, but the choir has outstanding carved walnut stalls and there is a handsome 18th-century altar behind it. A door in the south wall leads to a sunny little Renaissance courtyard, brimming with shrubs and flowers.

✉ Plaza de la Catedral 🕐 Mon–Fri 10–5, Sat 10–1 💶 Inexpensive 🍴 Bodega Montenegro, Plaza Granero (€€) 🚌 Parque de Nicolás Salmerón

LAS ALPUJARRAS

Best places to see, ➤ 24–25.

COSTA TROPICAL

The Costa Tropical is the westward
extension of the Costa de Almería, and
occupies Granada province's Mediterranean
shoreline. It is less developed than its
neighbour and has some spectacular rocky
coastline, a number of pleasant beaches and
attractive resorts such as Almuñécar and
Salobreña. Almuñécar has fine Phoenician,
Roman and Moorish monuments. The
resort's beaches are pebbly and cramped,
but the stylish esplanade of Paseo Puerta
del Mar makes up for this.

🛡 124 E4 ✉ Adra to Almuñécar 🚌 Regular
service Almería–Málaga

GUADIX

Guadix is noted for its splendid cathedral
and for its remarkable cave dwellings. The
former dominates the heart of the town, its
red sandstone walls hiding a darkly Gothic
interior enlivened by baroque forms.
Opposite the cathedral's main doorway is an
archway leading to the Renaissance square
of Plaza de la Constitución, known also as
Plaza Mayor. From the square's far right-
hand corner go up steps and along Calle
Sant Isteban to reach a cluster of handsome
buildings including the Renaissance Palacio
de Peñaflor and its neighbouring 16th-
century church of San Agustín. Between the

two there is a seminary, through which you gain entrance to the rather down-at-heel Moorish Alcazaba. To the left of the Palacio de Peñaflor, in a sunken square, is the church of Santiago, with a fine Plateresque door frame.

Walk north from the Alcazaba to reach the Barrio Santiago, Guadix's famous cave district, where remarkable dwellings have been carved out of the soft tufa of tall pinnacles. Visit the **Cueva Museo** for an insight into the cave culture.

✚ 125 D5 ✉ 60km (37 miles) east of Granada 🚌 Granada–Guadix
❓ *Fiestas Patronales de la Virgen de la Piedad*, 6–15 Sep
ℹ️ Avenida Mariana Pineda ☎ 958 69 95 74

Cueva Museo (Cave Museum)
✉ Plaza del Padre Poveda 🕙 Mon–Fri 10–2, 4–6, Sat 10–2
✋ Inexpensive 🍴 Drinks kiosk (€) 🚆 Road train from town centre

MOJÁCAR

There are two Mojácars, and both are busy places. The old hilltop town of Mojácar Pueblo is hugely popular with the large number of visitors to Mojácar Playa, the straggling beach-side development that dominates the coast for several kilometres. Old Mojácar can still charm in spite of the summer crowds. Fight your way out of the central Plaza Nueva and its airy viewpoint of Mirador de la Plaza Nueva, and climb left to the little garden of Plaza del Sol, then on up to Plaza del Castillo for more exhilarating views. Head west from here to explore the narrow flower-bedecked streets and squares, with their excess of souvenir shops. After all this, the long narrow beaches of Mojácar Playa are easily reached.

✚ 125 E8 ✉ 65km (40 miles) northeast of Almería 🚌 Almería–Mojácar
❓ Moors and Christians Fiesta, 10 Jun; *Fiestas Patronales San Augustín*, 25–30 Aug ℹ️ Plaza Nueva ☎ 950 61 50 25

a drive around the Hills of Las Alpujarras

Take exit 164 off the Motril-Granada motorway (A44), signed La Alpujarra. Follow the road uphill until you are higher than the wind turbines on the hillsides. Lanjarón is the first town, the gateway to the Alpujarras. Follow the road through the town. At the first roundabout take the right exit for Órgiva to continue on the A348, then straight over the next roundabout as you leave Lanjarón. Continue on the A348 towards Órgiva. Before you enter the town turn left onto the A4132 to Trevélez. A petrol station stands just before the turning.

Continue to Pampaneira, ignoring all turn-offs. The landscape gets greener and more wooded up here. Before you reach Pampaneira you'll cross the Río Poqueira gorge. Pass through Pampaneira and take the next left signposted for Bubión.

Whitewashed Bubión, overlooking the gorge, is one of the most popular Alpujarran villages.

Beyond the next village, Campileira, the road peters out at the foot of Mulhacén.

Mulhacén is Spain's highest mountain at 3,480m (11,420ft).

Return downhill to the junction with the A4132 through the mountain towns of Pitres, Pórtugos and Busquístar, following signs to Trevélez and Ugíjar.

Beside the road, shops sell cured hams. You're entering the high Sierra Nevada and a view of Mulhacén's snow-streaked peak will fill your windscreen.

At Trevélez, the highest village in Spain, stay on the A4132 – the road veers right. At the top, follow the road to the left for Juviles, which becomes the A4130. At Juviles bear right and head downhill to the foot of the hill. Turn right, signposted Órgiva. At the next junction turn right again for Órgiva, rejoining the A348, which offers stunning views of Las Alpujarras.

The next village is Cádiar; keep left to stay on the A348 to Órgiva. At Órgiva, stay left, following signs for Lanjarón. At Lanjarón, turn left for the A44 Granada-Motil highway.

Distance: Approx 100km (62 miles) **Time:** 4 hours (excluding stops)
Start/end: Exit 164 off the Granada–Motril road (A44)
Lunch: La Artesa Restaurante (€€) ✉ Carretera de la Sierra 2, Bubión ☎ 958 76 34 37

MONTEFRÍO

This delightful village at the heart of olive-growing country is dominated by the Iglesia de la Villa, a splendid church on a craggy promontory. The other great building is the central Iglesia de la Encarnacíon, a circular neoclassical church, with a domed roof. Montefrío is famous for its sausages, and there are several good restaurants in which to sample them. There are also excellent local varieties of olives and olive oil. To the east, along the road to Illora, is the Neolithic burial site of Las Peñas de los Gitanos.

✚ 124 C3 ✉ 35km (22 miles) northwest of Granada 🍴 Café Bar La Fonda, c/ Amat 7 (€) 🚌 Regular service Granada– Montefrío

❓ *Feria de Verano,* 7–8 Jul; *Fiestas Patronales,* 14–17 Aug

NÍJAR

Ceramics and *jarapas*, light carpets and cloth goods, are specialities of this pleasant village at the foot of the Sierra Alhamilla. There are excellent pottery shops on Avenida García Lorca, the broad main street, and in Barrio Típico Alfarero, leading off from the far end of García Lorca. As always in Andalucían villages, however, you need to go a little further to find the very special places. Walk on from the top of García Lorca past the

tourist office and then up Calle Carretera to the church of Santa María de la Anunciación, which has an excellent *artesonado* coffered ceiling (a panelled timber style of Moorish origin). Keep on to the left of the church, cross Plaza de Granero and continue up Calle Colón, past the covered market, to reach the wonderful Plaza del Mercado, with its overarching elm trees and striking Fuente de la Villa de Níjar, the blue-tiled public fountain with gaping fish-head faucets. Finally leave the top right-hand corner of the square to find, at Lavadero 2, La Tienda de los Milagros (the 'Shop of Miracles'), selling some of the finest ceramic work you could hope to find.

➕ 125 E7 ✉ 30km (19 miles) northeast of Almería 🍴 Café Bar La Glorieta (€€) 🚌 Regular service Almería–Níjar

SORBAS

Sorbas is the village of the *casas colgadas*, the 'hanging houses', a picturesque term that sums up its dramatic clifftop location above a dry valley. There is a strong tradition of pottery-making: the main workshops are in the Barrio Alfarero, in the lower part of the village. The central square, the Plaza de la Constitución, is flanked by the church of Santa María and the old mansions of the dukes of Alba and Valoig. The plaza's central fountain sports the heads of fierce beasts, their mouths crammed with water faucets. As you wander through Sorbas, you will emerge at various *mirador* viewpoints above the cliffs. The village lies at the heart of the Parque Natural de Karst en Yesos, a dramatic limestone landscape.

➕ 125 E8 ✉ 40km (25 miles) northeast of Almería 🚌 Regular service Almería–Sorbas ❓ *Fiesta Cruz de Mayo*, 1–3 May. *Fiesta San Roque*, 14–17 Aug. Guided tours of nearby Cuevas de Sorbas (Sorbas Caves ☎ 950 36 47 04 💧 Expensive) are available
ℹ Santa Terraplén 9 ☎ 950 36 44 76

Málaga and Cádiz Provinces

The provinces of Málaga and Cádiz are the most popular of Andalucían destinations – mainly because of Málaga's mass tourism venue, the Costa del Sol, but also because of their spectacular landscapes, old Moorish villages and historic cities and towns. Both provinces have some of the most remote inland and coastal areas in Andalucía. Málaga boasts the remarkable mountain areas of El Torcal and the Sierra Ronda. The Atlantic coast of Cádiz has emptier beaches, and in the north of the province there are

Cádiz

Málaga

spectacular mountain areas, such as the Sierra de Grazalema.

Málaga city has outstanding monuments and a reassuring sense of everyday Andalucían life. Cádiz city has the same authenticity, with the extra magic of its rich history. Fascinating provincial towns, such as Ronda and Jerez de la Frontera, and a host of intriguing villages add to the rich rewards offered by these most southerly provinces.

MÁLAGA

Málaga lies handsomely between the mountains and the sea. It is a busy, friendly city, relatively untouched by the conspicuous tourism of the crowded Costa del Sol, despite being the transit centre for most beach-bound visitors from Northern Europe. The city has lost some of its style through excessive development, but its major monuments, such as the Moorish Alcazaba and its subdued but intriguing cathedral, survive. Many historic buildings have been restored. Beautiful churches, the Museo Picasso, which opened in 2003, and other fine museums, fashionable shops, an excellent mix of bars and restaurants and a persuasive Mediterranean climate all add to Málaga's charm.

Málaga city lies on either side of the Río Guadalmedina, an arid trench for most of the summer. To its west lie large swathes of modern development and what is left of the old district of El Perchel. East of the river, the broad, tree-lined avenue Alameda, the main axis of the city and home to numerous flower stalls, leads to the busy traffic junction of Plaza de la Marina. Beyond it is the delightful Paseo del Parque, a palm-shaded promenade complete with a botanical garden and lined with some fine buildings. Look for the bronze sculpture, The Jasmine-Seller, as you stroll in the mellow Málaga evening.

South of the Alameda, a dense block of buildings robs the main city of views to the harbour and to the sea. North of the avenue is the commercial centre, where the area around the market on Calle Atarazanas preserves much of the atmosphere of the old city. East of here are the busy shopping streets that radiate from the lively and diverting Plaza de la Constitución, from which the main street of Calle Larios links the centre with Plaza de la Marina.

Scattered throughout the main centre are many bars, cafés and restaurants, where you can enjoy Malaga's distinctive cuisine, including its famous fried fish. A few steps east from the Plaza de la Constitución lie the attractive streets and plazas of the historic cathedral district. Above the city is the Alcazaba, on its stepped hill that rises even higher to the Castillo de Gibralfaro.

✚ 123 E5 ✉ 219km (131 miles) from Seville

ℹ Pasaje de Chinitas 4 ☎ 952 21 34 45

La Alcazaba

Málaga's Alcazaba has a wonderful sense of antiquity in its rough walls and in the maze of terraces, gardens, patios and cobbled ramps that lead ever upwards through impressive archways into the sunlight. The lower part of the Alcazaba dates from the 8th century, but the main palace is from the 11th century. Málaga's long history is reflected in the partly excavated Roman theatre, below the entrance to the Alcazaba, and in the various marble classical columns embedded within the dark brickwork of the fortress. The upper palace contains the small Museo de la Alcazaba, which displays Moorish artefacts recovered from the site and vicinity, amid decorative patios and rooms. There are magnificent views of Málaga from the ramparts.

➕ 126 E2 ✉ c/ Alcazabilla s/n
☎ 952 12 88 30 🏛 Museo de la Alcazaba: Tue–Sun 9:30–8
✋ Inexpensive; Sun free after 2pm
🍴 El Jardín, c/ Canon 1 (€–€€)
🚌 35

Casa Natal de Picasso

You cannot fault a city whose most famous son was one of the world's greatest painters, Pablo Ruiz y Picasso (1881–1973). The Casa Natal de Picasso (Picasso's Birthplace) is the headquarters of the Picasso Foundation, and is located in a handsome terrace of 19th-century houses in the large and friendly Plaza de la Merced, with its big central memorial. The building is significant more for its sense of Picasso's presence than for its rather spare (though elegant) rooms, converted out of Picasso's early home. There are some fine mementoes and photographs of the artist, not least the striking photograph in the entrance foyer.

🚩 126 E1 ✉ Plaza de la Merced 15 ☎ 952 06 02 15 🕐 Daily 9:30–8
✋ Free 🍴 Several cafés in Plaza de la Merced (€)

Castillo de Gibralfaro

The much-renovated Moorish Castillo de Gibralfaro (Castle of Gibralfaro) stands high above Málaga and above the Alcazaba, to which it is connected by a parapet wall. There are exhilarating views from the

ramparts and from the terraced approach path that leads up from the Alcazaba amid a mass of bougainvillaea and flower beds – but hang on to your wallet or handbag.

🚩 126 F3 ✉ Monte del Faro ☎ 952 22 72 30 🕐 Daily 9–7:45
✋ Inexpensive 🍴 Parador de Málaga Gibralfaro (€€€) 🚌 35 from Paseo del Parque. Horse-drawn carriages also make the trip from the Paseo del Parque and from outside the cathedral

Catedral

Málaga's cathedral gets something of a bad press, due perhaps to its lack of a companion for its solitary tower. Another tower was planned originally, but was never constructed – the cathedral is known locally as La Manquita, or the 'one-armed woman'. Building work began in 1528 and was completed in 1783. The cathedral has a strong visual appeal, however, its dark, worn stonework making a pleasing contrast to the more modern buildings that crowd round it. Inside there is much Gothic gloom, in heavily marbled surroundings, with numerous attractive side chapels competing for attention. The *coro*, or choir, is the cathedral's great glory: its fine mahogany and cedar-wood stalls are embellished by carved statues of 40 saints. The adjoining church, the Iglesia del Sagrario, has a Plateresque doorway and a wonderful Renaissance high altar.

✚ 126 D2 ✉ c/ Molina Larios s/n ☎ 952 22 84 91 🕐 Cathedral: Mon–Fri 10–6, Sat 10–5:45. Iglesia del Sagrario: daily 9:30–12:30, 6:30–7:30 ♿ Inexpensive 🍴 El Jardín, c/ Canon 1 (€–€€)

Museo de Artes y Tradiciones Populares

This excellent museum is located in a restored 17th-century inn, the Mesón de la Victoria, built around a little courtyard.

On display is a host of traditional artefacts from the rural and seagoing life of old Málaga province, a rich reminder of a less frenetic age.

➕ 126 B1 ✉ c/ Pasillo de Santa Isabel 10 ☎ 952 21 71 37

🕐 Mon–Fri 10–1:30, 4–7, Sat 10–1:30. Closed Sun and public hols

✋ Inexpensive 🍴 El Corte Inglés Buffet Grill, Avenida de Andalucía (€)

Museo Picasso

The Picasso Museum opened in 2003. This splendid museum, housed in the handsome 16th-century Palacio de Buenavista, contains a collection of more than 200 Picasso works, including paintings, drawings, sculptures, engravings and some fine ceramics. Some archaeological remains can be viewed in the basement.

➕ 126 D2 ✉ Palacio de Buenavista, c/ San Agustin 8 ☎ 902 44 33 77

🕐 Tue–Thu 10–8, Fri, Sat 10–9 ✋ Moderate

More to see in Málaga and Cádiz Provinces

ANTEQUERA

Antequera has great charm behind its busy, unpretentious face. The main street of Infante Don Fernando is full of shops, lively bars and cafés. At its southern end is Plaza de San Sebastián and its church; it is here that old Antequera begins. Beyond the Plaza are the narrow streets of El Coso Viejo, through which the stepped Cuesta de San Judas leads to the Arco de los Gigantes, a 16th-century gateway to the Plaza Santa María and its church. There are exhilarating views from here. Steps lead from the Plaza to the ruined Moorish Alcazaba. On Antequera's northeastern outskirts, on the Granada road, is a group of impressive Neolithic-Bronze Age burial chambers, the Menga and Viera Dolmens.

✚ 123 D5 ✉ 38km (24 miles) north of Málaga
ℹ Plaza San Sebastián 7 ☎ 952 70 25 05

ARCOS DE LA FRONTERA

Arcos de la Frontera is one of Andalucía's liveliest towns. It has outgrown its Moorish hilltop settlement and now spills down from the craggy heights in a long, straggling tail of white buildings above the flat plain of the Río Guadalete. The older, upper part of Arcos is a maze of narrow streets that twist and turn round the churches of Santa María de la Asunción and San Pedro. The former dominates the Plaza del Cabildo, from whose *mirador* there are stunning views of the plain below.

✚ 122 D2 ✉ 50km (31 miles) northeast of Cádiz
🚌 Regular services Cádiz–Arcos, Jerez de La Frontera–Arcos ❓ *Semana Santa* (Holy Week), Mar/Apr; Easter bull-running; *Feria de San Miguel,* end Sep
ℹ Plaza del Cabildo ☎ 956 70 22 64

CÁDIZ

Cádiz captivates without even trying. This is one of the great historic ports of the Mediterranean, with a claim to being the oldest of European cities, and a distinctive peninsular site lending it immense character. The city was founded as *Gaadir* by the mineral-seeking Phoenicians, who exploited the tin and copper of the Sierra Morena. It was also an important port for the Romans and Visigoths. Under later Moorish control the city declined, and even today that distinctive Andalucían Moorishness seems absent from Cádiz. During the 18th century, the decline of Seville as a river port benefited Cádiz and the city became rich on the Spanish-American gold and silver trade.

Today there is a refreshing sense of easy-going life in the maze of streets and squares and along the great sweep of breezy seafront promenades. Tall buildings, salt-eroded and dark-stoned, enclose narrow, shaded alleys that open suddenly into great sun-drenched plazas and gardens and to the glittering Mediterranean. The main square of Plaza San Juan de Dios, with its handsome

Ayuntamiento (Town Hall) and its encircling bars and cafés, makes a lively introduction; and the morning market in Plaza de la Libertad is a blur of colour and movement. The city's splendid churches and museums, its fashionable shops and fine restaurants, its beaches and its flower-decked gardens all combine to make Cádiz a unique experience – even for Andalucía.

www.guiadecadiz.com; **www**.cadiz.es

✚ 122 D1

ℹ Paseo de Canelejas s/n

☎ 956 24 10 01; Avenida Ramón de Carranza s/n ☎ 956 25 86 46

Catedral Nueva

The massive New Cathedral is still under restoration but is open to the public – it is wise to check opening times before you visit. The building dates from the prosperous 18th century, and replaced the 'old' cathedral of Santa Cruz. The neoclassical main façade on Plaza de la Catedral is magnificent. It is crowned by a baroque dome, famously 'gilded' yet, in reality, faced with glazed yellow tiles. The interior of the cathedral is a gaunt, stone cavern, classically perfect. Below lies the claustrophobic crypt, which contains the grave of the musician Manuel de Falla.

✉ Plaza de la Catedral ☎ 956 28 61 54 🕐 Tue–Fri 10–1:30, 4:30–6:30, Sat 10–1 ⚡ Moderate 🍴 Café Bar La Marina, Plaza de las Flores (€€) 🚌 4

Museo de Cádiz

The Cádiz Museum is the pride of Cádiz and one of the best museums in Andalucía. The ground-floor collection is outstanding, especially the Roman displays. On the first floor are paintings by Roger van der Weyden, Murillo, Rubens and Zurbarán, and the top floor has displays of craftwork and a bewitching collection of traditional marionettes.

✉ Plaza de Mina 5 ☎ 956 20 33 68 🕐 Wed–Sat 9–8, Sun 9:30–2:30,
Tue 2:30–8 🍴 Cervecería Gaditana, c/ Zorilla (€€) 🚌 2 💶 Inexpensive; free
with EU passport

Oratorio de San Felipe Neri

Of all Cádiz's churches, the Oratorio de San Felipe Neri is the most
impressive. In March 1812 the building saw the temporary setting
up of the Spanish parliament, or Cortes, that proclaimed the first
Spanish Constitution – a radical document whose liberal principles
were to influence European politics as a whole. Plaques on the
outer wall commemorate leading Cortes deputies. Inside, two
tiers of balconies above exuberant chapels complement the high
altar and its Murillo painting, *The Immaculate Conception*, all
beneath a sky-blue dome.

The nearby Museo Iconográfico e Histórico (Iconographic and
Historical Museum) has a marvellous scale model of the late 18th-
century city, carved in wood and ivory.

✉ c/ Santa Inés 38 ☎ 956 21 16 12 🕐 Mon–Sat 10–1 💶 Inexpensive
🍴 Freiduría Las Flores, Plaza de las Flores (€€) 🚌 2

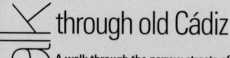

through old Cádiz

A walk through the narrow streets of the old town, seeing a remarkable church on the way.

From the far corner of the Plaza San Juan de Dios, to the right of the Town Hall, go along Calle Pelota and into Plaza de la Catedral. Leave by the far right-hand corner of the Plaza and go along Compaña to the busy Plaza de la Flores. Leave the Plaza to the left of the post office building to reach the market square, La Libertad.

The food market here is in full swing in the mornings.

Leave the market square along Hospital de Mujeres. Turn right along Sagasta and continue to Santa Inés. Go left here and pass the Museo Iconográfico e Histórico to reach the Oratorio de San Felipe Neri (► 91). From the church go down San José, crossing junctions with Benjumeda and Cervantes, then left through Junquería into Plaza de San Antonio.

This vast square is a pleasant place to relax in the sun.

Leave the Plaza on the same side as you entered, but go down Ancha, then go left along San José to Plaza de Mina and the Museo de Bellas Artes y Arqueológico. Take Tinte, to the right of the museum, to Plaza de San Francisco. From the square's opposite corner follow San Francisco through Plaza de San Agustín and on down Calle Nueva to Plaza San Juan de Dios.

Distance 2.5km (1.5 miles)
Time 3 hours, with visits to museums and churches
Start/End point Plaza San Juan de Dios
Lunch El Madrileño (€–€€) ✉ Plaza de Mina

COSTA DEL SOL

Conspicuous tourism is the business of the Costa del Sol, the long ribbon of holiday resorts that runs from Nerja, east of Málaga, along its western shore to Manilva. A sun-seeking break on the Costa has been the aim of millions of tourists over the years and the Costa has responded with gusto.

Resorts such as Marbella and Puerto Banús have an upmarket image and prices to match, while mid-range resorts like Torremolinos, Fuengirola, Benalmádena Costa and Estepona cover a variety of styles, from 'outgoing' to 'retiring'. All sum up the sea, sun, sand and sangría image. Smaller resorts, such as Sotogrande and San Pedro de Alcántara, now merge with the seamless concrete of the Costa. You will find more Englishness than Andalucían here, but for a good beach holiday, the Costa del Sol is still hard to beat.

✚ 123 E6 ✉ Between Nerja and Gibraltar 🍽 El Portalon, Carretera Cádiz, Km 178, Marbella (€€€); many other bars, cafés and resturants along the coast (€€–€€€) 🚌 Regular service from Málaga to all resorts 🚆 Regular service Málaga–Torremolinos–Fuengirola

GIBRALTAR

The wide open spaces of the airport approach to Gibraltar emphasize just how spectacular the famous 'Rock' is. This is the genuine point of contention between Spain and Britain, steeped in nautical history. Gibraltar has been a British colony since 1704 and, although its populace has evolved into an engaging mix of British-Mediterranean character, the buildings, culture, style and especially the commerce are emphatically British. There is enough in Gibraltar to make a visit enjoyable apart from the fascination of the mighty rock: its famous apes, the cable car, St Michael's Cave and views to Africa. Passports must be shown at the police and customs post.

✚ 122 F3 ✉ 120km (75 miles) southwest of Málaga 🚌 Daily Cádiz–La Linea, Málaga–La Linea; regular service La Linea–Gibraltar

GRAZALEMA

Mountains define Grazalema. They loom like clouds above the village and fill the distant horizon. This is the heart of the Parque Natural Sierra de Grazalema, a spectacular area of harsh limestone peaks softened by vast swathes of the rare Spanish fir, the *Pinsapo*, as well as by cork and holm oak. The *Parque* is a superb walking and rock-climbing area, and is reputed to have the highest annual rainfall in Spain.

The impressive peak of San Cristóbal towers above Grazalema. In the central square, Plaza de Andalucía, is the attractive church of Nuestra Señora de la Aurora. There is a fountain with amusing faucet heads to the side of a little lane called Agua, which leads to a flower-filled patio ringed by café-restaurants. The craft shop above the tourist office sells locally made produce.

✚ 122 D3 ✉ 20km (12 miles) west of Ronda 🍴 Cádiz El Chico, Plaza de España (€€) 🚌 Daily Ronda–Grazalema ❓ *Feria de Grazalema,* 22–25 Aug 🛈 Plaza de España ☎ 956 13 22 25

JEREZ DE LA FRONTERA

Best places to see, ➤ 28–29.

MEDINA SIDONIA

Nothing could be more detached from seagoing than this quiet hilltop town on the edge of the Parque Natural de los Alcornocales, yet Medina Sidonia was the ducal home of the admiral who led the Spanish Armada in its disastrous attack on Britain.

The tree-lined main square, the Plaza de España, is overlooked by the Ayuntamiento (Town Hall). At a shop here, or at the Convento de San Cristóbal in Calle Hercules 1, you can buy some of Medina's famous *dulces* (sweet cakes), such as the almond-flavoured *alfajores*. In the upper town, the church of Santa María la Coronada, in the sunny Plazuela de la Iglesia Mayor, has a very fine altarpiece; behind it are the remains of a Moorish Alcazar. From the Plazuela, a path leads to hilltop views of the surrounding countryside of La Janda.

➕ 122 D2 ✉ 30km (18 miles) east of Cadíz 🍴 Mesón Bar Machín, Plaza Iglesia Mayor 9 (€€) 🚌 Regular service Cadíz–Medina Sidonia

NERJA

These days Nerja is firmly established as part of the Costa del Sol. It is an enjoyable though busy resort with pleasant beaches, and is famed for its Balcón de Europa, a palm-lined promontory on the old belvedere of an original fortress. There is an appealing freshness about Nerja but the form of the old town survives in

its narrow streets. It can be crowded, however, especially at weekends, but it maintains a relaxed air. The cool interior of the simple church of El Salvador, by the Balcón de Europa, reflects this detachment. The best beaches, Calahonda and Burriana, lie to the east of the Balcón. The popular limestone caves, the **Cuevas de Nerja**, lie about 4km (2.5 miles) east of the village.

123 E7 52km (32 miles) east of Málaga Several cafés and restaurants (€–€€€) Daily Málaga–Nerja, Almería–Nerja
Carnival, Feb; *Cruces de Mayo*, 3 May; *Virgen del Carmen*, 16 Jul
Puerta del Mar 4 952 52 15 31

Cuevas de Nerja

4km (2.5 miles) east of Nerja
952 52 95 20;
www.cuevadenerja.es Summer daily 10–2, 4–8; winter 10–2, 4–6:30
Moderate Restaurant on site (€€) *Festival de la Cueva* (flamenco and classical music), Jul

RONDA

The dominant feature of picturesque Ronda is the deep gorge (El Tajo) of the Río Guadalevín. Between its towering walls a handsome 18th-century bridge, the Puente Nuevo, hangs like a wedge, groaning beneath the massed weight of visitors. On the south side of the bridge is the old Moorish town. Its focus is the Plaza Duqueza de Parcent, where the fine Iglesia de Santa María Mayor stands on the site of an original mosque. Other places to visit south of the gorge include the Palacio de Mondragón in Calle Manuel Montero, the Minaret de San Sebastian in Calle Armiñan, the Iglesia del Espíritu Santo close to the Puente Nuevo, and the Arab Baths near the Puente Viejo, or Old Bridge, to the east.

On the north side of the Puente Nuevo is the Mercadillo district of modern Ronda. Halfway along Calle Virgen de la Paz is the famous bullring, opened in 1785. It was here that Pedro Romero established the rules of fighting bulls on foot. The attached museum is full of bullfighting memorabilia. From opposite the bullring, stroll up Carrera Espinel, the pedestrian-only main shopping street, where you will be spoiled for choice.

✠ 122 D4 ✉ 118km (73 miles) northwest of Málaga 🚆 Málaga–Ronda 🚌 Regular services Málaga–Ronda, Seville–Ronda ❓ *Samana Santa* (Holy Week), Mar/Apr; *Feria y Fiestas de Pedro Romero*, 31 Aug–10 Sep (traditional bullfighting)

ℹ Plaza de España 1 ☎ 952 87 12 72

TARIFA

Tarifa is Europe's most southerly point. Africa is within reach: the blurred outlines of the Moroccan mountains loom across the Strait of Gibraltar, only 14km (9 miles) away. It was at Tarifa that the Moors gained a first foothold on *al-Andalus* in 710. Tarifa is often swept by fierce winds from the stormy bottleneck of the Strait, where the Mediterranean and Atlantic meet head-on. Today, its once remote beaches have been reinvented as world-class venues for windsurfing. You can dodge the wind amid the wriggling lanes and tiny squares and patios of Tarifa's walled Moorish quarter where, in Plaza de San Mateo, the 15th-century Iglesia de San Mateo has a glorious Gothic interior with rich baroque elements. Head west from Tarifa to some of the finest, if often breeziest, beaches around, or visit the impressive Roman ruins at Baelo Claudio, 14km (9 miles) along the coast towards Cádiz (guided visits only).

www.tarifaweb.com

🛧 122 F2 ✉ 90km (56 miles) southeast of Cádiz 🚌 Daily Málaga–Tarifa, Cádiz–Tarifa ❓ *Fiesta de la Virgen de la Luz,* 6–13 Sep

ℹ️ Paseo de la Alameda s/n ☎ 956 68 09 93

VEJER DE LA FRONTERA

The hilltop settlement of Vejer de la Frontera preserves its Moorish character, with an enchanting maze of narrow streets and an old Moorish castle.

🛧 122 E1 ✉ 42km (26 miles) southeast of Cádiz 🚌 Regular services from Cádiz–Vejer. Málaga–Cádiz buses stop on main road below village. From here, 4km (2.5-mile) steep walk, or taxi

ZAHARA DE LA SIERRA

Best places to see, ➤ 40–41.

Seville and Huelva Provinces

Andalucía's most westerly provinces of Sevilla (Seville) and Huelva are precisely defined by the hills of the Sierra Morena in the northwest and by the fertile plain of the Río Guadalquivir, La Campiña, in the southeast. The Sierra Morena is the least-populated part of Andalucía, and although these hills lack the spectacular ruggedness of other ranges, their tree-covered slopes and scattered villages have an appealing remoteness. The region's coastline is contained mainly within Huelva province and includes the great delta of the Guadalquivir and the Parque Nacional de Doñana.

Seville lies at the heart of the region. This is Andalucía's capital and

its most fashionable city, home to magnificent monuments and with a cultural life to match any city in Europe. Huelva city is a more mundane, workaday place, fuelled by industry, but with some fine churches and museums.

SEVILLE

Seville is one of the most exciting cities in Europe. It is crammed with elegant shops, bars and restaurants, yet within the old quarter of the Barrio Santa Cruz lies a tangle of shaded alleyways, plazas and patios of almost village-like character. The great monuments of the cathedral, the Giralda and the Reales Alcázares apart, Seville has numerous other superb attractions. The vibrant cultural and social world of the city spills over into almost every aspect of life, mixing the very best of the past with modern elegance and fashion.

Seville generates style and romance like heat from the sun. Think Carmen and Don Juan and you have some measure of the city's passionate, if sometimes theatrical, character. Yet there is an easy-going element about Seville that is essentially of the Mediterranean.

The city evolved as a historic trading centre for the gold and silver of the Sierra Morena. It was controlled by the Romans and then by the Moors from 712 until the Christian Reconquest of 1258. The discovery of the Americas made Seville one of the greatest ports and cities in Europe. Decline came with the silting of the Guadalquivir, but the legacy of this era remains to this day.

Seville's main focus is its magnificent cathedral and Giralda tower (► 104–105) and the adjacent Alcázar (► 36–37). The cathedral and La Giralda are among the most visited monuments in Europe, but the weight of people does not diminish the fact that these are stunning buildings. South of the cathedral, beyond the Avenida de la Constitución, is the commercial district. Northeast of the cathedral is the delightful old Jewish quarter of Barrio Santa

Cruz (➤ below), while a little farther north is one of Seville's hidden gems, the 16th-century mansion La Casa de Pilatos (➤ 104), claimed to be based on Pontius Pilate's house. Southeast of the cathedral are the public spaces of Plaza de España and the María Luisa Park. To the north lie the bustling Plaza de San Francisco and the great canopied shopping street of Calle Sierpes and its neighbours.

www.turismosevilla.org

➕ 118 D4

ℹ️ Avenida de la Constitución 21 ☎ 954 22 14 04

Barrio Santa Cruz

A first experience of the tightly knit alleyways of the Barrio Santa Cruz can seem claustrophobic. Tall buildings shut out the sun; their stonework is dark and gloomy; the mood seems more northern European than Andalucían. But the Barrio eventually captivates. Santa Cruz was the *aljama*, or Jewish quarter, of the medieval city and was greatly changed after the Jewish community was expelled in 1492. The area was much restored and refurbished in the first years of the 20th century, and its narrow, muffled streets are a wonderful antidote to the raging traffic of Seville's busy main thoroughfares. Wander at will and you will soon discover flower-filled corners such as Plaza Santa Cruz, the Jardines de Murillo on the Barrio's eastern boundary and the Plaza Doña Elvira. There are numerous bars and cafés along the way.

➕ 127 B3 ✉ East of the cathedral

🍴 Bars, cafés and restaurants (€–€€€)

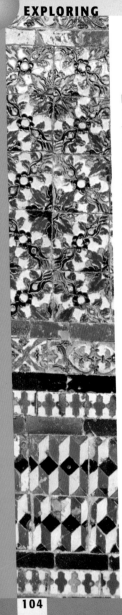

La Casa de Pilatos

Pilate's House is one of Seville's finest treasures. Built in 1519, the house was said to be a copy of Pontius Pilate's house in Jerusalem, but there is no real evidence confirming this. The entire building is a glorious celebration of the Mudejar style mixed with the most elegant of Italianate features. The *azulejos* tiling is outstanding; the patios, arcades, stairways and richly furnished salons are all superb. This is the best place to truly get a feel for the subtle complexities of this unique architecture. There is hardly a finer self-contained complex of late medieval style and design in Andalucía.

✚ 127 A3 ✉ Plaza Pilatos 1 ☎ 954 22 52 98
🕐 Summer daily 9–7; winter daily 9–6 ✋ Expensive
🍴 Bodega Extraména, c/ San Esteban (€€) 🚌 C1, C2, C3, C4 (for Plaza San Agustín)

La Catedral y La Giralda

Seville's cathedral is said to be the largest Gothic church in the world. It replaced a mosque, and was a gesture of unashamed Christian triumphalism following the Reconquest. The cavernous interior seems almost too vast to express anything other than empty pride, but the magnificent altarpiece in the sanctuary, intense focus of countless guided groups, is breathtaking in its exuberant design. The choir and Renaissance Capilla Real (Royal Chapel) are just as striking. Outstanding works of art and religious artefacts fill the cathedral, and the alleged tomb of Christopher Columbus makes an eye-catching theatrical piece.

You can climb the Giralda – although at busy times tackling the tower's 34 ramps and 17 final steps becomes something of a weary trudge. The Giralda is the surviving 12th-century minaret of the original mosque, a structure that was heightened in 1565 by the addition of a bell tower and crowned by a bronze weather vane (*giraldillo*). The tower's exterior is its true glory, but the views from its upper gallery are impressive.

www.catedraldesevilla.es

🕂 127 B2 ⊠ Plaza Virgen de los Reyes ☎ 954 21 49 71 🕗 Summer Mon–Sat 9:30–4, Sun 2:30–6; winter Mon–Sat 11–5, Sun 2:30–6 🍽 Numerous restaurants in c/ Mateos Gago (€–€€€) 🖐 Moderate; free Sun 🚌 Avenida de la Constitución

Itálica

The Roman ruins of the city of Itálica lie 9km (5.5 miles) north of Seville and can be reached by bus from the city's Plaza de Arma bus station.

➕ 118 D4 ✉ Santiponce ☎ 955 99 65 83 🕐 Closed Mon and festivals

Museo del Baile Flamenco

Seville's Museo del Baile Flamenco, which opened in 2006, is dedicated to the dance that touches every facet of the city's character: flamenco. The museum prides itself on its interactivity; there are frequent workshops in the basement, where you can learn the basics. On the upper levels there are costume displays, video shows and photographic exhibitions. What the museum imparts is a passion for flamenco, which, after all, is exactly what the dance is about.

www.museoflamenco.com

➕ 127 A2 ✉ c/ Manuel Rojas Marcos 3 ☎ 954 34 03 11 🕐 Apr–Oct daily 9–7; Nov–Mar daily 9–6 ✋ Moderate 🚌 Avenida de la Constitución

Museo de Bellas Artes

The Fine Arts Museum, in the beautiful old convent La Merced Calzada, is one of Spain's major art galleries. Highlights are works by Zurbarán and Murillo, including the latter's *Virgin and Child*, the famous 'La Servilleta', so named because the 'canvas' is said to be a dinner napkin. There are other works by Goya,

Velázquez and El Greco. Room 5, once the convent church, is dazzling, with its painted roof and collection of works by Seville-born master Murillo.

🚩 127 A2 ✉ Plaza del Museo 9 ☎ 954 78 65 00 🕐 Tue 2:30–8:30, Wed–Sat 9–8:30, Sun 9–2:30 💷 Inexpensive; free with EU passport 🚌 C3, C4, C5, 6, 43

Plaza de España and María Luisa Park

Semicircular Plaza de España is fronted by a short length of canal, spanned by ornamental bridges. María Luisa Park is a glorious stretch of wooded gardens, abundant in flowering plants. Beyond are the Museo Arqueológico and the Museo de Artes y Costumbres Populares (Popular Arts Museum).

🚩 127 C3 ✉ Avenida de Isabel la Católica

Reales Alcázares

Best places to see, ➤ 36–37.

More to see in Seville and Huelva Provinces

ARACENA

Aracena's most lauded attraction is the limestone cave complex, the Gruta de las Maravillas (Grotto of Marvels, ➤ 26–27). But Aracena and its surroundings have much else to offer. The town surrounds a hilltop medieval castle ruin and its adjacent church of Nuestra Señora de los Dolores; there are pleasant bars and cafés in the surrounding streets.

www.aracena.es

➕ 118 C4 ✉ 89km (55 miles) northwest of Seville 🍴 Several (€–€€)
🚌 Daily Seville–Aracena, Huelva–Aracena
ℹ St Pozo de la Nieve ☎ 959 12 82 06

AROCHE

The hilltop village of Aroche lies only 24km (15 miles) from the border with Portugal. Its Moorish castle, established in the 9th century, was rebuilt substantially in 1923 and now incorporates one of Andalucía's most eccentric bullrings, as well as the village's archaeological museum. Ask for permission to obtain access at the Town Hall if the castle is closed. Just below the castle is the peaceful church of Nuestra Señora de la Asunción. Aroche's main square, Plaza de España, is a delightful place to linger over a drink.

✚ 118 B3 ✉ 33km (20 miles) west of Aracena 🍴 Bars and cafés in main square (€) 🚌 Daily Aracena–Aroche ❓ *Semana Santa* (Holy Week), Mar/Apr; Pilgrimage of San Mamés, Whitsun; *Feria de Agosto*, Aug; Pilgrimage, Jun

CARMONA

Carmona stands on an escarpment overlooking the fertile valleys of the Río Corbones and the Río Guadalquivir. Over 4km (2.5 miles) of ancient walls enclose old Carmona, and the main entrances to the town are through magnificent Roman gateways, the Puerta de Sevilla and the Puerta de Córdoba. The lively Plaza de San Fernando has some fine buildings, and nearby is the market.

Follow narrow Calle Martín López de Córdoba out of Plaza de San Fernando to reach Santa María la Mayor church. The church is entered through the delightful Patio de los Naranjos, the entrance patio of the mosque that originally stood here, still with its orange trees and horseshoe arches. The church has a soaring Gothic nave and powerful *retablo*. Uphill, Calle G Freire leads to the superbly located Alcázar del Rey de Pedro, now an exclusive *parador*.

The Seville Gate incorporates the Moorish Alcázar de Abajo, now home to Carmona's tourism office. Beyond the gate, across the busy Plaza Blas Infante, is modern Carmona, with its handsome church of San Pedro, whose great tower replicates the style of Seville's Giralda. A wide and busy promenade leads to Carmona's Roman Necropolis, one of Andalucía's most remarkable archaeological sites.

www.turismo.carmona.org

✚ 119 D5 ✉ 38km (24 miles) east of Seville

🛈 St Arco de la Puerta de Sevilla

☎ 954 19 09 55

ÉCIJA

This Ciudad de las Torres (City of Towers) has a dramatic skyline. Eleven magnificent church towers, steepled, domed and exquisitely decorated with colourful tiles, punctuate the sky, each with its resident storks. The town is much more than its towers, of course. There are remarkable 18th-century façades, so fluid in their forms that they hint at the 19th-century work of architect Antoni Gaudí. Track down the Palacio de Peñaflor in Calle Castellar. It is a remarkable building, painted and sinuous and with a flamboyant baroque portal, lacking only a wider street to set if off. The Palacio de Benameji in Calle Cánovas del Castillo, home to a town museum, is another delight. Écija's splendid central square – the Plaza Mayor, or Plaza de España – has been walled off for the construction of an under-ground car park, which has robbed the encircling arcades and cafés of light and air; all the more reason to admire the glorious church towers.

www.turismoecija.com

🚩 119 E7 ✉ 80km (50 miles) east of Seville 🚌 Daily Seville–Écija ❓ *Semana Santa* (Holy Week), Mar/Apr; *Feria de Primavera* (Spring Fair), 8 May
ℹ️ Sq de Espana 1 ☎ 955 90 29 33

HUELVA

Huelva is the fourth-largest port in Spain. The city has paid a price for centuries of industry and commerce. Yet its heart has great charm and life. The palm-fringed main square, Plaza de las Monjas, is surrounded by busy streets. A short distance east along the arcaded Avenida Martín Alonso Pinzón, in Alameda Sundheim, is the impressive Museo Provincial. Northeast is the curious Barrio Reina Victoria, or the Barrio Inglés, an Anglicized complex of housing, a legacy of the Río Tinto company.

➕ 118 D2 ✉ 90km (56 miles) west of Seville 🚉 Estación de Ferrocarril, Avenida de Italia ☎ 902 24 02 02 🚌 Estación de Autobuses, Avenida de Portugal 9 ☎ 959 25 69 00
ℹ Plaza Alcalde Coto de Mora 2 ☎ 959 65 02 00

MOGUER

Moguer is one of the smartest and friendliest towns in Andalucía. The pretty central square, Plaza Cabildo, has a superb neoclassical Town Hall, framed by palm trees. Opposite, in a little square, there is a bronze bust of Juan Ramón Jiménez, a native son and a Nobel Prize-winning poet. A museum dedicated to him is at his birthplace, Calle Jiménez 5. The 14th-century Convento Santa ClaraIn, in nearby Plaza de las Monjas, is a museum and art gallery with a Mudéjar-style cloister and delightful church, still used for worship. Adjoining it is the splendid Convento de San Francisco.
www.aytomoguer.es

➕ 118 D2 ✉ 15km (9 miles) east of Huelva 🚌 Regular service Huelva–Moguer
ℹ Castillo s/n ☎ 959 37 18 98

through the Sierra Norte

a drive

**This drive takes you through the lesser-known parts
of Seville province: the remote Parque Natural de la
Sierra Norte.**

*Leave Carmona by the Seville Gate and follow signs for
Lora del Río on the A457. After 20km (12 miles), go left at
a junction. Cross the Río Guadalquivir and the railway
line, then go left on the A431 to a junction before Alcalá
del Río. Take the first exit (signed C433 Burguillos and
Castilblanco). Stay on the C433 to Castilblanco, then
follow signs for Cazalla de la Sierra on the C433.*

You are now entering the Parque Natural de la Sierra Norte. The road winds through lonely hills swathed in cork oak, holm oak, pine and chestnut. Vulture, eagle and black stork are found here, and deer, wild boar, wild cat and mountain goat haunt the woodlands and rocky tops.

At a junction with the A432 go left (signed El Pedroso). At El Pedroso go right at a roundabout (signed A432 Constantina, Cazalla de la Sierra). Cross the railway and follow signs to Cazalla.

Cazalla de la Sierra is a pleasant country town, famous for its cherry brandy.

Leave Cazalla from its northern end, following signs for Constantina on the A455. Drive through wooded countryside, cross the railway at the isolated Constantina station and continue to Constantina.

Constantina is dominated by the medieval Castillo de la Armada, on a high hill, and has a charming old quarter.

Continue south from Constantina on the A455 to Lora del Río. Re-cross the railway line, then retrace your route back to Carmona.

Distance 220km (135 miles)
Time 8 hours, with stops
Start/end point Carmona ✚ 119 D5
Lunch Restaurante del Moro (€) ✉ c/ Paseo El Moro, Carmona ☎ 954 88 43 26

Index

Acknowledgements

The Automobile Association would like to thank the following photographers, companies and picture libraries for their assistance in the preparation of this book.

Abbreviations for the picture credits are as follows – (t) top; (b) bottom; (c) centre; (l) left; (r) right; (AA) AA World Travel Library.

4l La Alhambra, Granada, AA/J Edmanson; **4c** Reales Alcázares, Seville, AA/A Molyneux; **4r** Plaza de España, Seville, AA/D Robertson; **5l** Nerja, AA/M Chaplow; **5c** Velez Blanco, AA/D Robertson; **6/7** La Alhambra, Granada, AA/J Edmanson; **10/11** Children at a festival, AA/D Robertson; **13t** Seville Airport, AA/A Molyneux; **13b** Carriage driver at the Mezquita in Córdoba, AA/D Robertson; **14/15** Taxi rank, AA/A Molyneux; **17t** Postbox, AA/M Chaplow; **17c** Telephone box, AA/M Chaplow; **18** Policeman, AA/J Tims; **20/21** Salon of the Ambassadors, Reales Alcázares, Seville, AA/A Molyneux; **22** La Alhambra, Granada, AA/D Robertson; **22/23** La Alhambra, Granada, AA/D Robertson; **24/25t** Las Alpujarras, AA/D Robertson; **24/25b** Bubión, Las Alpujarras, AA/D Robertson; **26/27** Gruta de las Maravillas, MELBA PHOTO AGENCY/Alamy; **28** Royal Andalusian School of Equestrian Art, Jerez de la Frontera, AA/P Wilson; **28/29** Jerez de la Frontera, AA/J Edmanson; **29** Jerez de la Frontera, AA/M Chaplow; **30/31** La Mezquita, Córdoba, AA/D Robertson; **31** La Mezquita, AA/M Chaplow; **32** Parque Natural el Torcal, AA/M Chaplow; **33** Sierra del Torcal in Parque Natural el Torcal, AA/M Chaplow; **34** Detail of Fuente del Rey, AA/M Chaplow; **34/35** Fuente del Rey, AA/M Chaplow; **35** Whitewashed house, Priego de Córdoba, AA/ M Chaplow; **36** Reales Alcázares, Seville, AA/A Molyneux; **36/37** Reales Alcázares, AA/A Molyneux; **38** Sacra Capilla del Salvador, AA/M Chaplow; **38/39t** House in Úbeda, AA/M Chaplow; **38/39b** Church of Santa María de los Reales Alcázares, AA/M Chaplow; **40/41** Zahara de la Sierra, AA/M Chaplow; **42/43** Plaza de España, Seville, AA/D Robertson; **45** Baeza, AA/M Chaplow; **46** Waterfall at Alcázar de los Reyes Cristianos, AA/M Chaplow; **47** Alcázar, AA/M Chaplow; **48/49** Alcázar, AA/M Chaplow; **50** Baeza, AA/M Chaplow; **50/51** Roman church, Baeza, AA/M Chaplow; **51** Baños de la Encina, AA/M Chaplow; **52** Cazorla, AA/M Chaplow; **52/53** Jaén, AA/M Chaplow; **54/55** Segura de la Sierra, AA/M Chaplow; **56/57** Segura de la Sierra, AA/M Chaplow; **58/59** Waterfall at Río Guadalquivir, blickwinkel/Alamy; **60** Velez Blanco, AA/D Robertson; **61** Velez Blanco castle, AA/J Edmanson; **62/63** The Albaicín, Granada, AA/M Chaplow; **64/65** Capilla Real, Granada, AA/ D Robertson; **65** Capilla Real, Granada, AA/M Chaplow; **66/67** Convento de San Jerónimo, Granada, AA/M Chaplow; **68** Plaza Nueva, Granada, AA/M Chaplow; **70/71** Almería, AA/D Robertson; **72/73** La Alcazaba de Almeíra, AA/J Edmanson; **74/75** Salobreña, AA/J Tims; **75** Guadix, AA/M Chaplow; **76/77** Las Alpujarras, AA/D Robertson; **78/79** Iglesia de la Encarnación, Montefrío, AA/M Chaplow; **79** Níjar, AA/M Chaplow; **80** Flamenco show 'Corral de la Morerie', AA/M Jourdan; **81** Ronda, AA/P Wilson; **82/83** View from Castillo de Gibralfaro, Málaga, AA/J Tims; **84/85** La Alcazaba, Málaga, AA/P Wilson; **85** La Alcazaba and Castillo de Gibralfaro, Málaga, AA/P Wilson; **86t** Málaga Cathedral, AA/M Chaplow; **86b** Museo de Artes y Tradiciones Populares, AA/J Poulsen; **86/87** Museo de Artes y Tradiciones Populares, AA/J Poulsen; **88/89** Cádiz, AA/P Wilson; **90** Cádiz Cathedral, AA/P Wilson; **91** Oratorio de San Felipe Neri, Cádiz, AA/D Robertson; **93** Cádiz, AA/J Edmanson; **94/95** Gibraltar, AA/P Wilson; **96** Church of Santa María la Coronada, AA/M Chaplow; **96/97** Balcón de Europa, Nerja, AA/J Tims; **98/99** Ronda, AA/D Robertson; **99** Tarifa, AA/P Wilson; **100** Barrio Santa Cruz, Seville, AA/P Wilson; **101** Plaza de España, Seville, AA/D Robertson; **102/103** Plaza de España, Seville, AA/P Wilson; **103** Barrio Santa Cruz, Seville, AA/M Chaplow; **104** La Casa de Pilatos, AA/P Wilson; **104/105** Seville Cathedral, AA/J Edmanson; **106/107t** Plaza de España, Seville, AA/J Edmanson; **106/107b** María Luisa Park, Seville, AA/J Edmanson; **107** Tile in Plaza de España, Seville, AA/D Robertson; **108** Aracena, AA/D Robertson; **108/109** Aracena, AA/D Robertson; **109** Carmona, AA/D Robertson; **110/111** Écija, AA/D Robertson; **111** Huelva, AA/D Robertson; **112/113** Seville Gate, Carmona, AA/M Chaplow.

Every effort has been made to trace the copyright holders, and we apologise in advance for any accidental errors. We would be happy to apply the corrections in the following edition of this publication.

Maps

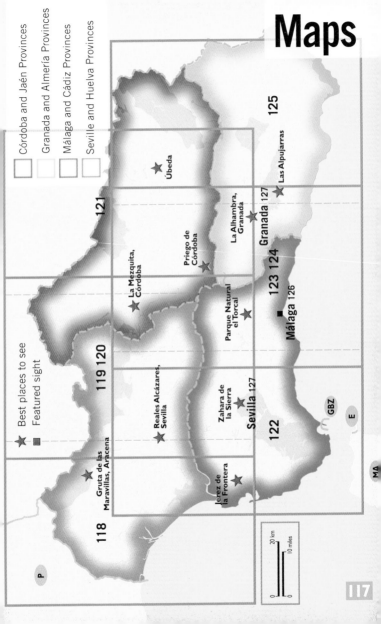

Córdoba and Jaén Provinces

Granada and Almería Provinces

Málaga and Cádiz Provinces

Seville and Huelva Provinces

★ Best places to see

■ Featured sight

118

Gruta de las Maravillas, Aracena ★

119 120

Reales Alcázares, Sevilla ★

Jerez de la Frontera ★

121

La Mezquita, Córdoba ★

Úbeda ★

Priego de Córdoba ★

Parque Natural el Torcal ★

La Alhambra, Granada ★

Granada 127

Las Alpujarras ★

125

123 124

Málaga 126 ■

Zahara de la Sierra ★

Sevilla 127

122

GBZ

E

MÁ

P

20 km

10 miles

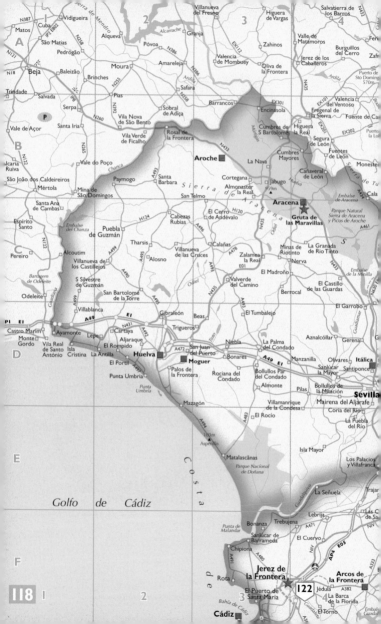

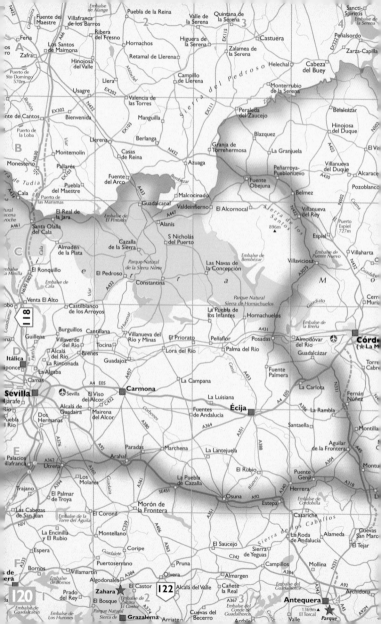

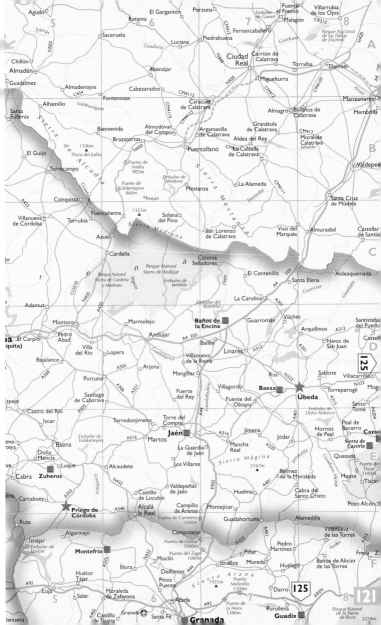

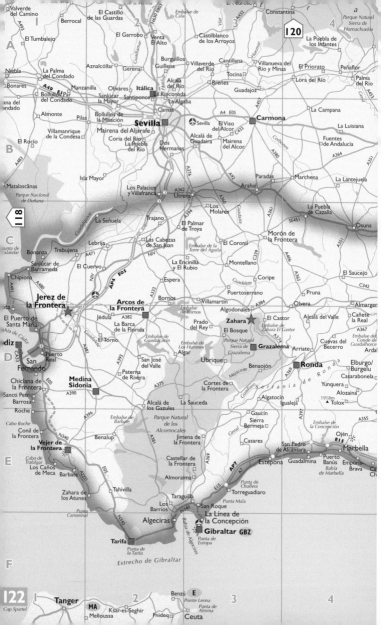

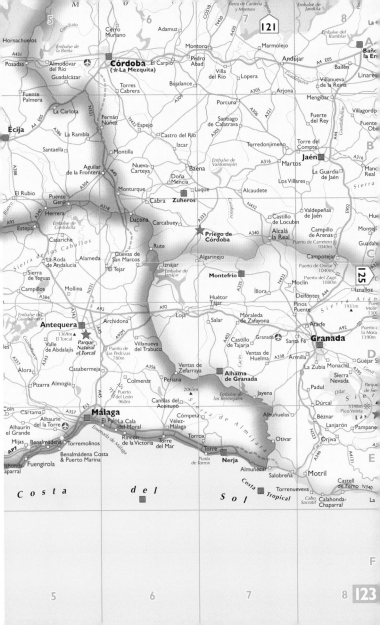

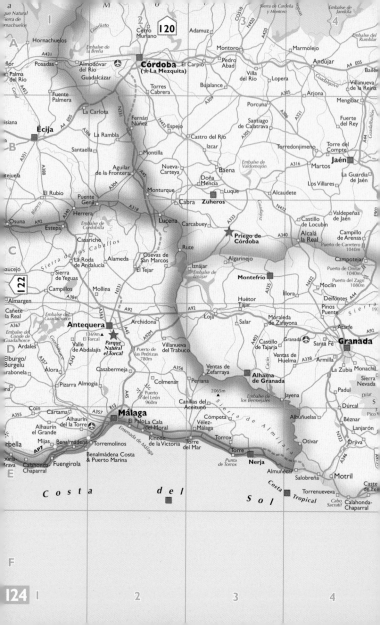

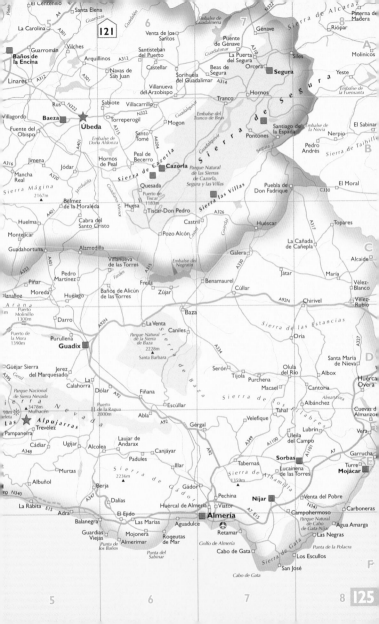

Málaga

Castillo de Gibralfaro

Casa Natal de Picasso

La Alcazaba

Museo Picasso

Catedral

Museo de Artes y Costumbres Populares

CENTRO

Centro de Arte Contemporáneo de Málaga

Plaza de la Victoria

Calle del Agua

CRUZ VERDE

GÓMEZ SALAZAR

LAGUNILLAS

LA VICTORIA

FRAILES

H DEL CONDE

Clemens

Plaza Santa María

MARIBLANCA PEÑA

Hinestrosa

MADRE DEL DIOS

CALLE ÁLAMOS

MUNDO NUEVO

Plaza de la Merced

Santa Ana

Plaza de Santiago

Iglesia de Santiago

ALCAZABILLA

CASAPALMA

Calle de Beatas

SAN AGUSTÍN

GRANADA

Plaza Uncibay

Plaza del Teatro

COMEDIAS

CISTER

Teatro Romano

Palacio de la Aduana

PASEO DEL PARQUE

El Parque

PASEO DE ESPAÑA

DEL MUELLE

SANTA MARÍA

LARIO

ABADES

Plaza Obispo

MOLINA

CORTINA

SANTA LUCÍA

Dulces

Cabello

Iglesia de los Mártires

Iglesia del Sto Cristo de la Salud

Plaza de la Constitución

Plaza de Consititución

BOLSA

Plaza de las Flores

MARQUÉS DE LARIOS

Plaza de la Marina

ARCO de

Santos

PTA NUEVA COMPAÑIA

CISNEROS

NUEVA

Iglesia de San Juan Bautista

Gigantes

Plaza F. Sáenz

ALARCÓN LUJÁN

M García

MARTÍNEZ

CARRETERIA ÁLAMOS

Murgia

PASILLO SANTA ISABEL

MARQUÉS

PASEO ATOCHA

Mercado Central

ATARAZANAS

PLAZA DEL MAR

ALAMEDA PRINCIPAL

CÓRDOBA

GRUND

DE HEREDIA

TOMÁS

DE

CAMPOS

VENDEJA

TRINIDAD

Casas de

Barroso

M CAMPOS

ALMEDA DE COLÓN

AVENIDA DE MANUEL AGUSTÍN HEREDIA

Muelle de Heredia

CERROJO

Aq Parejo

Santo Domingo

Plaza de Trinidad

Cañaveral

ARMENGUAL DE LA M

del Obispo

Almansa

CALVO

CALLE HILERA

Santa Rosa

Puente de Tetuán

Estación

Museo de la S Santa

Río Guadalmedina

GUILLÉN SOTELO

Ayuntamiento

AVENIDA CERVANTES

Hospital

PASEO REDING

Plaza de Toros

Muelle de Guadiaro

Muelle de Guadiaro

Sevilla

SANTA JUSTA

C S Laureano
C. Alfonso XII
C de Laraña
Imagen
C. JOSE LAGULLO
C RECAREDO

AV. CRISTO DE LA EXPIRACION
Museo de Bellas Artes
C. San Eloy
C. SIERPES
Cuna
Santiago
Navarros
C Imperial
C. Marqués de Paradas
Albareda
Museo del Baile Flamenco
Casa de Pilatos
C. LUIS
MONTOTO
C. Blanco White
C. Juan de Zoyas
C. Mallén

CALLE ZARAGOZA
Castelar
C. Adriano
C. San José
Pelayo
C. JOSE MARIA MORENO GALVAN
Granada
C. Jiménez
C. Pirineos

PASEO CRISTOBAL COLON
PLAZA DE LA CONSTITUCION
Catedral y la Giralda
Barrio de Santa Cruz
C. Agua
AV EDUARDO DATO
B

CALLE PAGES DEL CORRO
Betis
C. Alfarería
Plaza de Toros de la Maestranza
Hospital de la Caridad
Reales Alcázares
C. Catalina de Ribera
C. MENENDEZ
C. Capitán Viqueras
AV DE LA BUHAIRA
Barrau

CALLE
Luna
Febo
C. Correa
Torre del Oro
AV CARLOS V
C ENRAMADILLA
AV RAMON Y CAJAL
C. Avión Cuatro Vientos

AV BLAS INFANTE
C. Trabajo
Salado
Virtud
CALLE
Niebla
C. Bdet
Elcano
AV REPUBLICA ARGENTINA
C. Juan Sebastián
Turia
Arcos
Canal de
AV MARIA LUISA
Av Portugal
C. Isabel la Católica
Calle Doctor Pedro Castro
C Ramón Carande
C. Santa Rosa

Parque de los Príncipes
C. Padre Damián
C. Virgen del Águila
ASUNCION
Calle Juan Ramón Jiménez
Alfonso XIII
LAS DELICIAS
AV. Magallanes
Parque de María Luisa
Plaza de España
C San Salvador
C. porvenir
CALLE FELIP II
300 m
300 yds

Granada

Monasterio de la Cartuja

Jardines del Triunfo
AV DEL HOSPICIO
de
C. San Luis
C. del Agua
Calle Pino
C. Panaderos
C. San Cecilio
Calle Pages
D
200 m
200 yds

AV DE LA CONSTITUCION
C. Aceitia Casteros
C. de Dios
Calle de la Alhacaba
Carril de la Lona
C Santa Isabel la Real
Pilar Seco
C Tiña
Callejón de San Agustín
Carril de San Agustín
Ctra Abadía del Sacromonte
Chapiz

Monasterio de San Jerónimo
SAN JUAN
Gran
Via
Calle
Mano de Hierro
C de San José
Quilada
Albaicín
Museo Arqueológico
C de San Gregorio
Santísimo
Cuesta
Cuba
C Zafra
Paseo del Padre Manjón
Cta de Rey Chico
E

C ALONSO CANO
C. Duquesa
C. San Jerónimo
C. Santa Paula
Malaga
Cta de Aranidas
Cta de Maranas
C. Aire
C San Juan de los Reyes
Carrera del Darro
Baños Arabes
Casa de los Pisas
La Alhambra

Buenseceso
C ALHONDIGA
C. Gracia
Mesones
C. Cárcel Baja
Colón
Oficios
Cárcel
Catedral & Capilla Real
Alcaicería
La Madraza
Plaza de Bib-Rambla
Corral del Carbón
Cta de Gomérez
Cta de Gomérez
Paseo de los Mártires

Cuesta de la Magdalena
Cruz
C. Varela
Escudo del Carmen
C ANGEL GANIVET
C SAN MATIAS
C. SANTA ESCOLASTICA
C. SANTA PALACIOS
C. Aire Alta
Callejón Niño del Royo
Plegadero Bajo
C ANTEQUERUELA BAJA

Titles in the series